MW01181587

"Discover the How-To Secrets of Planning Your Wedding Entertainment"

All The **Tips & Tricks** No One Else Will Ever Tell You To Eliminate Your Stress And Help You Sleep Like A Baby Leading Up To Your **Fun And Exciting** Wedding Day

By:

Sgt. Steve Preston Zuelzke
www.TheWeddingEntertainmentGuru.Com

MSI Publishing, Inc.
and
Sound Advice Music and Entertainment

Other Readers Are Already Saying . .

"At Last! - - - A Guidebook to Ensure You a Happy and Successful Wedding Reception Free of Worry and Stress"

"The advice, suggestions, and information in this book will help you make good decisions as you prepare for your wedding reception. It's an easy read with many well-thought out ideas. This will allow you, and your guests to enjoy a very special event. The bride and groom will be **free of the trivial details** and you will be pleased and proud with how your reception flows if you follow this book. Just use the great information in this Guidebook to plan your memorable day with DJ Entertainer, Sgt Steve Preston Zuelzke."

**Nancy Knutson
Duluth, GA**

Other Readers Are Already Saying . .

"If You Stumbled Upon A Wedding Reception Guide, Which Offered You The Secrets To A Stress-Free Event This Book Does, Would You Be Savvy Enough To Follow the Lead?"

"After reading this book, I want every couple getting ready marry to know of the resources covered in this book. If you are looking for a way to take the stress out of planning your wedding reception, then this book will help you. It is a great tool to help you plan and prepare for your once in a lifetime event by offering you a guide and path to walk down with Sgt Steve Preston Zuelzke as your valuable partner and expert resource. Don't leave the starting line alone!"

John Caterer
Bloomer, WI

"The Secret to a Successful Wedding Reception is Selecting the Right DJ Entertainer at the Beginning"

"After reading this book, I now see how selecting my DJ Entertainer right at the start is the key to a successful night. This book lays out your options and your need-to-know items so you ask all the right questions."

Teri Royer
Neenah, WI

Published 2016 by:
Sound Advice Music and Entertainment
W3178 Van Roy Road
Suite D # 150
Appleton, WI 54915

In 2016 in conjunction with:
MSI Publishing Inc.
Thomas F. Ribar
Michael J. Dickow
262-375-7400 or Tom.msipub@Gmail.com
Grafton, WI 53024-1764

DISCLAIMER AND/OR LEGAL NOTICES:

Printed in the United States of America

A Ringing Endorsement

A Long-Time Associate of Sgt. Steve Preston Zuelzke Recognizes Steve's Professionalism, Experience and His Ability to Make it All Look So Effortless

Mark Whipp Congratulates Steve on His Completion of This Desperately Needed Book for the Wedding Reception Industry

❝ Having been a family owned and operated business for almost 95 years and hosting weddings and other events for 75 of those years, here at Eddie Whipp's we think we have seen it all. I have been the owner here for the past 35 years and worked with Steve for close to 20 of those years. It has been easy to recommend Steve to our wedding couples as he is always professional and keeps the party going. He has tons of experience making a seemingly complicated job look so effortless.

Over the years we have had the opportunity to work with many different wedding vendors. In order for us to suggest a vendor to any of our clients they need to have all of the credentials and Steve definitely has that and much more! I will be easily recommending Steve and Sound Advice for the next 35years. ❞
Thanks Steve.

Mark Whipp,
Owner
Eddie Whipp's Supper Club and Banquet Hall

Acknowledgments

I want to start by dedicating this book to my late wife Kerry who supported me through thick and thin during my career. You gave me the motivation and the drive to take on writing this book in addition to all the other things I was trying to get done. I know you would be proud of all the work I put in to get this book completed. Thank you my dear.

Secondly, I want to thank all my friends and their families for allowing me to follow my passion for DJ Entertainment from a very young age. I also want to thank my parents for putting enough faith in their 14 year old to let me buy my first set of DJ equipment. And, I want to thank my sisters for allowing me to listen to your records so I could get a good understanding of different types of music. It was like having instant access to my own iTunes library before there was such a thing.
I also want to thank my grandparents for having the confidence to hire a young kid to entertain at their adult events and gain valuable live experience. Thank you all for your love and support throughout my blossoming career right from the start.

I would like to thank everyone who helped and supported me throughout the designing and creating of this book. And without your enthusiastic support of my DJ Entertainer dreams, as an upstart, I would never have been able to meet and work with so many wonderful brides and grooms. It is your life lessons along the way, which have been invaluable in getting me to where I am today in this most challenging and competitive industry. It is each one of you, the brides and grooms whom I have met along the twisting and turning road of life, who have helped me become the DJ Entertainer I am today, and given me the credibility and reputation to author this book.

6

Very special thanks also go out to three extra special people. Without any one of them, my career in the world of DJ Entertainment, and then this book, would never have gotten off the ground. First a big thanks to my mentor in the DJ business, Jim Bernard Hebel. Jim took a chance on me in my 20's and gave me my first opportunity to be on the radio. Jim mentored me in the early days of my own DJ Entertainment business and his mentorship has helped Sound Advice to become the success it is today. Thanks Jim.

And then, and very significantly, I want to thank Thomas Ribar and Mike Dickow, my editor, publisher and co-author team. It is only because of their mentorship, you are reading this book. The ideas Tom and Mike provided really opened my eyes as to why creating and writing this book in the first place would be a real life saver to brides and grooms everywhere.

Their inspiration meant everything to me and helped me create a book to be even more than I could imagine beyond my wildest dreams. From developing the details to what it might look like all the way to what you have in your hands today, they were instrumental every step of the way.

I am sure they did a lot behind the scenes to make this dream of mine come true which I am not even aware of, and that's OK with me. I can't thank them enough for all of the conference calls, meetings, long nights all of the work they put into this project. The road had many twists and turns but they always made sure I kept my eye on the target.

If you ever want to get a book written, published or even just completed, these are the "go-to" guys for sure. They can get it done for you.

Thanks a bunch guys!

TABLE OF CONTENTS

About the Author.. 11

Forward

Why Am I Writing this Book 16

Don't Be a Wedding Reception Victim 21

Bonus - Getting the Most Out of this Book 25

Chapters

1) Saying Thank You by Celebrating With Family and Friends 39

2) Check for Conflicting Events on <u>Your</u> Date 49

3) Select the Proper Venue – It's a Balancing Act 55

4) Compare Your Entertainment Options 67

5) Accept Only the Best for Your Wedding Entertainment (You Deserve it!) 81

6) Budget for the Right Entertainment – The Plan Starts With the Right Numbers 95

7) Go See Your Entertainment in Advance - Know Who AND What You Are Getting 115

8) Stay Away From the Entertainment Handyman 133

9) Entertainer Accreditation? -- Real Nonsense! 139

10) Working Through a Talent Agency? -- Attention to Detail is Critical 145

11) Sign the Contract – Success Requires It! 153

12) Your DJ Knows Their Equipment . . . Or Do They? 159

13) Room Layout -- Why Should I Care? 169

14) If A Theme Is Important, Go With It!! 181

15) The Ultimate Forget Me Knot Wedding Planner™ -- Your "How-to" Planner for Your Perfect Stress-Free Wedding Reception 187

16) The Ultimate Wedding Review™ -- Your Final Review Discussion to go Over Every Detail of the Wedding Reception 201

17) The DJ Entertainer Assessment 217

      People **219**
      Process **220**
      Products **222**

Appendix

♦ Hear it from Others – More Happy Brides and Grooms **226**

♦ See it From Others Point of View **231**

♦ Book Index **234**

♦ Order Your Resources: (3 Items) ....

1. Discover the How To Secrets of Planning Your Wedding Entertainment - **Book** **240**

2. Wedding Reception Secrets Quick Start Toolkit **242**

3. "12 Wedding Reception Courtesies You Need to Know!" – **Book** **244**

♦ Contact the Author – Sgt. Steve Preston Zuelzke **246**

♦ Your Monthly Drawing **248**

♦ Sgt Steve Preston Zuelzke is Available For You ...

....**250**

About The Author

Hello, my name is Sgt. Steve Preston Zuelzke. My passion for music and entertaining started very early in my childhood when I was barely 6 years old. I've presented myself as a formal DJ entertainer since I was 14. Yes, I started quite early.

When I was only in 8th grade I purchased my first real DJ music system for $3,000.00. Back in those days this was a whole lot of money. I had built my business up, which included being the DJ at my first wedding, and actually getting paid for it, in 1978. I was both an eager and aggressive guy. I did pretty well if I do say so myself and it helped I was a pretty good saver.

Over the next two years I built a reputation as one of the "most reliable" and "hottest" DJ's in the Fox Valley Area (Appleton, WI). Even to this day a DJ at 16 years old rocking an adult dance floor is unheard of. I advanced my night club business to become the entertainment director and DJ for several night clubs in the Fox Valley area.

As I reflect on my career, I firmly believe it was the "most-reliable" label, hung on me at an early age which has served me the best as I grew up.

I wanted to advance in to the world of radio, but I could not get a station to hire me. I figured I needed more credentials so I enrolled in the Trans American School of Broadcasting. Here I obtained my Associates degree in Radio and TV Broadcasting.

It was at this point where I finally realized my dreams when I was hired at KCHA, an AM/FM station in Charles City, Iowa. I was thrust into the evening DJ role to start but it was only a matter of a few days before I was given the keys to the coveted morning drive-time spot. I rewarded the trust of the station manager by having the number 1 ratings in the local area after two and half years. Part of my reward was being promoted to Program Director for all 5 radio stations in their "family" of stations. After a while in Iowa, I got a yearning to return home so in 1992 I moved back to Appleton, WI. It is

Never Underestimate Just How Important Your DJ Entertainer is to the Success of Your Reception

Steve-
Right after the Minister and bride, you were the most important person at our wedding. Thanks so much for your help Steve!!!

Mike and Kathy

here where as Sgt. Steve Preston, I created the **Sound Advice Music and Entertainment** business.

For over 30 years, I have been helping brides and grooms throughout Wisconsin and the Midwest throw unforgettable receptions. I have attempted to build a strong reputation on being THE most reliable DJ in the business. I pride myself as a professional who does far more than just show up and just play music. Although we will have a contract if you choose to work with me, I believe my word and my handshake would be good enough because you can count on me to do what I promise. If you are a bride or groom getting ready for your big day then I would be pleased and proud if you would allow me to become your trusted resource in planning your wedding reception.

People describe Steve as:
"The perfect mix of Fun, Entertainment and Professionalism, all wrapped up in one person – and that is tough to find. Sgt Steve is your Guy!"

Why Sergeant Preston?

Many people ask me the story behind the name so please allow me to provide you the details right here.

When I first moved to Iowa, to be on the radio, the news guy at the radio station gave me the nickname of <u>Sgt. Preston of the Yukon</u> because he said I looked like him. Since I didn't even know who <u>Sgt. Preston of the Yukon</u> was, I had to go to the local library (no internet in those days) to research who this guy was. I found out he was actually a pretty kool guy in law enforcement and even had a husky by the name of King.

I tried to fight the name at first but I liked the similarities, slowly became attached to it and it ultimately stuck.

When I moved back to Wisconsin, I shortened it to Sgt Steve Preston and eliminated the Yukon part. To this day many people just call me Sarge. The real Sergeant in my life, however, is my father, a retired CSM (Command Sergeant Major) of the WI National Guard-32nd Red Arrow Division. And that's the rest of the story!

Steve Was Attentive to Detail Which Helped Every Person Have the Best Time They Could

Dear Steve,
Thank you so much for making our wedding ONE BIG PARTY!!! We had a blast and so did our guests. Many of our friends and family have told us it was the best time they have ever had at a reception. We couldn't have done it without you.

Sincerely,
Cory and Emily

Sgt Steve Will Create Such a Fantastic Event You Will Never Be Afraid To Recommend Him Time and Time Again to Your Friends

Steve,
Thank You so much for the awesome DJ work at our wedding! The dance floor was packed the entire night and I got so many compliments on you and your talent. Thanks again for the recordings. We listen to them all the time. We would definitely recommend you to anyone!

Thanks Again,
Becky and Ryan

Forward

Why am I Writing This Book?

I decided to write this book because so many books in the past have tried to scare, you, the reader with all the stories of what has gone wrong at wedding reception events – you know the big mistakes, the huge slip-ups and gigantic oversights. I decided I did not want to write a book with all the bad or negative stories. It is not only too easy to do but it has been done way too many times before. There are also many web sites and wedding magazines where these stories are collected for your amusement.

And on top of all of this, I take great issue with the all too many unprofessional and unscrupulous people in our entertainment industry who, quite frankly, can too easily mess up your reception event with these type of stories. They're only interested in the money because this type of story sells like hotcakes and really do nothing to help you get it right. I want to help you turn your binoculars around to the other direction, to where you want to go, not to where you've been or to where you don't want to go. Let's quit with the negative thoughts and start with the positive thoughts of how to do it right. How does this sound for a change? Are we together? OK?

I want to help you look forward – to see what needs to be done in a positive light to create the best possible, stress-free (Yes – Stress-Free!) wedding reception event you want for your wedding. Because in the end, isn't that what YOU want, the route to get it done - - - - right? Of course it is!

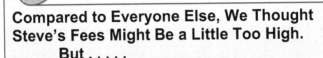

Compared to Everyone Else, We Thought Steve's Fees Might Be a Little Too High. But . . . . .
In the End, ...
We Realized What Tremendous Value Steve Provided Every Step of the Way

Sgt. Steve Preston was amazing to work with. From the very beginning he does his best to get back to you the moment he has a chance to breathe. Phone calls and emails were the easiest way to contact him.

During the wedding there was some small confusions regarding name pronunciations and a song change for the father-daughter dance, but those minor issues were swept away with each song. Steve stayed up on the stage the entire night, keeping people on the dance floor over and over again. He honored our do not play list, and played as many songs as he could from our preferred list.

I strongly suggest Sgt. Steve Preston. His costs were reasonable, and we truly enjoyed working with him. To . . . . . anyone looking for a DJ, he is your man!

My book is filled with advice for both couples and event planners—it's a roadmap you can use to ensure your event is memorable, fun and stress free – with a heavy emphasis on the stress-free!

I know this book is going to go against what you may have heard and may have read in other typical wedding magazines and wedding planner articles. This book is sure to ruffle some feathers in the wedding and event planner industry. Why?

Simply because I am going to tell it like it is and give you all the tips and tricks I have learned in my many years in the wedding entertainment business. It's time to get the truth out in the open without any hidden agendas. You see, I have nothing to hide. I never have. It's just I am finally taking the time to put it all down in writing so I can share it with you.

From Entertainer to Party Go'er in One Quick Phone Call – What Happened?

A number of years ago I had a friend of mine call me to be the DJ at his wedding, I accepted . . . .
Several weeks later he called me back to cancel the same booking. He said another friend of his had a son who was in college and had just started to DJ for extra money, and his son was less than half my fee. So he felt obligated to hire him instead. As a friend I did not give him too hard of a time over this short term cancellation because I was still invited to attend as a wedding guest. I did try to warn him of the potential issues which could arise, but he politely told me how his wife-to-be was really the decision maker on this budgetary item this time and money appeared to be the ruling force.

Curiosity Won Out –
I Went to the Wedding Anyway

I was not very interested in going to this wedding, as I attend plenty of them. Believe me. However, my curiosity got the best of me, so I decided to go to the wedding anyway and check things out. When I arrived at the country club, the DJ was on top of the head table. He sat slouched in a chair, had sunglasses on along with his headphones. He had brought in his home stereo system and was playing Punk, Grunge and Classic Hard Rock music during cocktail hour - - - at quite a loud volume. People of all ages were complaining like crazy. My friend, the groom, (who remember was NOT the decision maker on this hire), asked if I would try to talk some sense into this young man (kid) for him, as he wasn't listening to anyone. I was a bit apprehensive but I said, "OK I'll give it a whirl."

Steve Goes Out of His Way to Please
<u>Every Bride and Groom</u>

Steve,

Thank you so much for all your help in making our wedding reception perfect! It really was!!! You did an amazing job of keeping our guests on the dance floor all night. Thank You Again for staying that extra hour too!! We really needed it, my family just wasn't ready to let the party end at midnight.

Thanks Again,
Kyle and Erica

When I approached the DJ he tore his headphones off and started to raise his voice and swore and told me to get away from him. He was yelling at me, "You're just jealous I got the gig and not you."

I tried to calm him down so I could say something. He put his headphones back on, slouched back in his chair, assuming his original position and continued rocking to the music. Oh well. I thought. I tried. I went back to the groom and told him I had no success and he simply has the wrong guy.

The groom then asked me "What am I supposed to do now?" I replied, "I don't know."

The groom stated, "I guess I have to live with it." In a nutshell the dinner music got worse and by the time the dancing was to start the hall was almost deserted. My friend came up to me and explained how he had thought he had saved a lot of money but in the end he really hadn't saved a thing because the event turned out to be a disaster.

The reality is; the majority of entertainment in your area is going to end up just like this unless you know what questions to ask, up front. And, note, here is a good example of how the least expensive alternative is not always the BEST alternative. I am going to prepare you with all the right questions for each situation in this book. Just follow along and you will see each checklist and each set of questions presented as you need them. And of course I have a very easy way for you to get them too.

Start by accepting you will need to do some simple review questions (or homework questions) at the end of each chapter. Learning does not take place simply by reading. You probably remember hearing this back in school at least several times. Well, it's still true today. One still needs to push the pencil to really learn and remember anything, even today.

And simply selecting the <u>cheapest</u> entertainment is NOT the answer either. The "cheapest route" will result in a horrible event 99% of the time. Spending the right money on your entertainment won't guarantee a **Good Entertainer** either because some companies or services will disguise themselves with a high price. This is why doing your homework prior to selecting your entertainment is so important. There is no need for you to learn this lesson in person. You can save a lot of time and money, mostly your precious time, by reading and doing the activities in this book.

Don't Be a Wedding Reception Victim

By following the simple steps you will learn from this book you will gain the confidence in who you hire to be your DJ entertainer and ensure you won't be the next victim. You will hire the right person to make your day a guaranteed success.

I've even seen so called DJs purposely sabotage a wedding reception event so they could go home early. They play music they know will purposefully thin the crowd on the dance floor for the evening. Then - - - what happens you ask? What would YOU DO? Don't think too long on this one. - - -

Yes, you're right. "You would start heading for the exits too, right?"

No one asks or will hold the company responsible for their actions, because they are being paid for the evening, not hourly, and the public doesn't know any better. I think these actions are a travesty and nobody should ever have to put up with a person they hire who has purposely ruined their event. **(Certainly not YOU, because now you're aware of what's actually going on with these <u>purposeful</u> and <u>fraudulent</u> actions)**

I Can't Help You <u>After</u> It's All Gone Wrong

I've received so many calls from clients disappointed by other entertainers. I guess they call me after their event because I have been in the business so long they feel I can do something for them. I can't. All I can say is, "It's too bad your event or wedding was ruined by someone with a great sales pitch." Your only recourse then is to look over the contract and call the company you hired or call the Better Business Bureau and file a complaint. If you had used my services, we wouldn't be having this conversation.

There's so much turmoil and frustration in this industry, and until now, there's never been a road map for a bride and groom or an event planner to follow.

That's Exactly Right. Never Until Now!!
But NOW There Is!!
You are among the first to have one right here in your hands!!

How Incredibly Exciting it is! And What a Great Decision you made to acquire this book at this time in your life.

I realized it was finally time to create a proven road map to help folks like you plan your once-in-a-lifetime memorable event.

The Purpose of This Book Is To Help You Way <u>Ahead</u> Of Time

I've been thinking about doing this book for a long while now. You won't believe some of the frustrating, unbelievable things I've seen. You, the public, are constantly being ripped off and victimized by rotten so called DJs, cover bands and talent agencies. I have so many stories to turn into lessons. Many can be funny when I look back on their frequency, although unfortunately not a single one of them has any humor in them for the people involved.

It will be up to us, as readers, many weeks and months later, to find the chuckle in them, and only when we have the advantage of "time" and "distance." Let me emphasize, and **only now**, have we earned the right to find the humor in the situation.

People deserve a great wedding reception or event, but it takes a little effort; a little planning on your part. A little research on your part ahead of time will help you hire the right person or group. Your event is then, going to turn out great! I promise.

Don't Let Distance Prevent You from Hiring The Best DJ Entertainer for Your Special Day!!!

Steve,
We cannot thank you enough for our wedding and everything you did to make it so special and memorable. You were incredibly easy to work with despite living so far away while trying to plan everything. Your excellent services and professionalism were key factors in making our special day go off without a hitch. I would definitely recommend you to anyone who is looking for a first-class party or event.

Thanks a million!!
Brandy and Matt

Getting the Most Out of This Book

My purpose in including this Bonus section for you is help you benefit from some powerful learning Tips I have used for years which help me read a book once and be able to refer to key passages later. This Bonus section contains some tips on how to read this book to **minimize your time** and **maximize the value** of the time you invest in reading the book. The goal is to help you make the best use of the time you have to invest in this book - - - and then of course to apply what you learn here to any other book you read in the future. These Tips are a Free Bonus I am providing you along with your investment in this book.

If You Are Already a Proven Speed-Reader . . .

If you are already a proven speed-reader or have your own tried and true technique for reading and taking good notes **then feel free to skip this Bonus section** and get started right away with Chapter 1. This Bonus section might give you a few tips you can add to your reading skill set but probably not make as big a difference on your wedding reception as the content of this book will.

What I mean is, if you are sure and confident in the success of your existing reading methodology, then planning your wedding reception should be much higher on your family priority list than improving your personal learning skills. (at least in my opinion.) So in terms of your time utilization right now, I recommend skipping this Bonus section and moving forward in this book to Chapter 1, the first content chapter, right now.

Let's Make Sure Our Goals Are In Sync

If, on the other hand, you have decided to take advantage of the Bonus section and invest the time to improve your book reading skills then we must make sure we are in sync with our goals for today.

When I find a reference book like this I want to <u>learn the most</u> but I also <u>want to invest the least amount of time</u> because it is not a novel that I want to get buried in. It's a book more like one I would be using in preparation to write a term paper back in my college or even high school days.

• • • **My Number One Goal is always to:**

<u>Read the Book Once!!</u>

I **take my notes** and **highlight what is important** to me on the **first reading** so I **never have to go back** to any parts other than the **key parts** ever again. Call me lazy but, I would rather you just say I am selfish and want to be efficient with my time.

Why do a job more than once if I can do it right the first time? I want to pass along my Tips to you about how I read a book once and be done with it – Period!! It's really as simple as that.

There are two parts here. The first part is stocking your toolbox with the tools you will need <u>before</u> you begin reading. The second part describes how to use the tools to enhance your reading.

<u>Let's stock your toolbox.</u>

1. Get a **good bright color highlighter (or two)**. You will want to able to highlight the key passages of text.

2. Next find **several colors of pens or pencils** you like so you can underline important areas and make notes in the margins of the book.

3. And third, you will need a pad of **Post-it note**™ **Tape flags.** These will allow you to label the pages where you have highlighted text or made notes in the margins.

4. And finally, if you are going to be reading this book on one of the multitude of <u>e-reader tools</u>, you will need to search out the most current version of one of the <u>support apps</u> which contain all of the electronic forms of the highlighter/under-liner tools I just described in items 1, 2 and 3 above. (and, you save money by not needing to invest in your own items 1, 2 and 3.) Yes, they do exist. Find the ones which work with your version of your e-reader. As an example, some basic highlighting tools are

already even built right into standard PDF files as this book goes to press.

I have seen some really powerful and slick capabilities at the app stores so get busy and get the app tool you need. Even if you are reading the book on your tablet, you still need to be highlighting and taking notes as if you had a hard copy version. The technology you use does not change the need to use these learning tools to help you easily and quickly understand via the use of these new apps. And, yes, the tools continue to improve are available for both the android and the apple platforms, and so far they have all been free.

There, now your toolbox is complete.

Why Do I Use These Special Tips?

1. They are simple.
2. I can do it at my desk.
3. I can use them on an airplane.
4. I can use them in a hotel room.
5. They have worked for me for years.
6. I use them all the time to great advantage and
7. So can you.

Now, let's dig in. The first thing is to . . .

. . . . Set Time Aside as a COUPLE . . .

. . to give this book some serious effort. The book is meant to be a casual read **for both** the bride and the groom.

Pick the Chapters Important to You – Then Focus

Of course, not everything in the book may be as applicable to your specific situation as other chapters, so you're going to have to pick the things you need to focus on. What do I mean by that? For example, if you are not going to use any video at your wedding reception, then don't invest too much serious time reading the chapter or sections on the etiquette and ideas for how to use video. I do, however, recommend still skimming over those areas lightly so you have it in your head for future reference. But certainly do not dwell on the chapters you know will not provide direct benefit for your upcoming event. Put your best efforts in the chapters where you can get the best leverage of your time for now. That only makes sense. Right?

This book is not written as a novel where you will be deeply engaged in character development in each and every chapter. This is meant to be a casual or a fun read.

When you and I get to meet in person along the road someday, you will find I am a fun guy and this book personifies who I am. If we have not yet met, I hope we do.

This book is, however, for the serious student who wants to get all the details of their wedding reception planned out in advance of the big day so they can *"sleep like a baby"* in the days and weeks leading up to the wedding. The book is for the kind of person who does not want to be running around town chasing down details at the last minute the day guests are arriving from out of town. If you would rather be hosting your guests and enjoying life as you lead up to the wedding day, then this book is for you.

There are no jokes in here. Some sections or chapters will be more interesting to you than others. But please take every idea and every suggestion seriously. They each come from years of experience and from seeing it in person. My goal is to help you avoid all the pitfalls I have seen others fall into, so you can plan the details of YOUR Stress-Free Wedding Reception. Got that? Get these details sorted out now and I guarantee you will be reducing a HUGE amount of the up front worry, sweat and Stress of the day because you are confident of your preparation.

You will have a chance to think through your entire wedding reception, on paper, in a matter of a days and hours. To be able to do this is truly powerful for you. Think about it. It may not seem so now, but at the conclusion of your reception day (maybe when you and your spouse are relaxing by the ocean at the resort on your honeymoon) you can look back with a big smile. Yes you are grinning from ear to ear when you look back on this early planning you did and you are ohhh soooo thankful because everything went off without a hitch.

After you complete this book, just step back and picture what an amazing and relaxing position you will be in prior to your wedding day. When you finish this book and complete each the action items you have identified, you will have solved all of the issues which other brides and grooms have found to be the "show-stoppers" and have gotten in the way of them having a successful and Stress-free wedding reception.

Think of what this means to you to have a plan and being able to visualize what your entire day will look like, in a compressed time frame, months in advance. Yes, you will have all the details figured out well in advance of your big day. Wow! What a relief that will be! Right?

Note: These are the same details other brides and grooms end up getting nibbled to death by because they forget them and do not know they need to address some of them until they are into the middle of the reception. And then the nibbles become an emergency! If only they had this book!

Here is The Best Way for You to . . .
1.   Read Once and be able to
2.   Reference Multiple Times

Let's get to step 2- Tips to read the book.
Now read the chapter and **As you are reading . . .**

1.   Look for anything; key points, ideas, action items
or to-do's pertaining to **Your Individual Situation**.
Some of us like to highlight these items. Others like to
underline in our favorite color pen. Whichever you
choose, just make sure you get it done, consistently in
each chapter. Mark what is most important to YOU and
your upcoming event!

Remember: Your goal is to read this book <u>ONCE</u>,
and highlight or underline this book <u>ONCE</u> so you do
not have to go back and read the entire book again.

2.   At the end of each chapter you will find a short
wrap up section labeled, "**Action Items**." This is where I
summarize the most important points of the chapter in the
form of several key points and/or questions. I want to
encourage you to invest the time **RIGHT NOW** . . . . .
while they are most fresh in your mind, and respond to
these questions or put down notes of what you need to do
to act on these key points from the chapter. Yes, Now!

3.   **Some answers or notes now are better** than no
answer at all. Even if you just jot down your initial
thoughts now and come back later to fill in the details,

that's great. This can be a good strategy. Responding to each of the **Action Items** will help you put structure to the chapter you just read before going on to the next topic in the next chapter. It helps you learn and most importantly makes sure your current thoughts and ideas are down on paper before you move on to the points of the next chapter. This helps me remember and I am confident it will help you remember as well.

Remember . . .

Step back for a moment - - - Please consider these **Action Items** to be

Your Nitty Gritty Steps for Success - - -

. . . and to help guarantee you consider each of the formal steps in a wedding reception and decide which apply to you, so you don't forget any at the last minute. This helps make your Wedding reception truly Stress-Free for you AND for everyone who is looking up to you with high expectations (i.e. especially all the parents, grandparents, etc). Again I emphasize Stress-Free here because it's what we are all after as one of our objectives for your wedding reception, right?

In some cases, your response to one of the **Action Items** might be an "educated" estimate. That's OK and it's far better than no response at all. If all we have is an educated guess right now, then this will be one of the places you'll need to come back to later to finish with a few more details. Not a big deal.

KEY POINT -- There is a reason these **Action Items** are pulled out and identified separately – THEY ARE based on what other brides and grooms have told me and from what I have experienced in hundreds of receptions over many years of experience. It is because of this history I am able to write with such confidence.

"Success Leaves Clues . . . (for you)
. . All Over the Place!!"

4.   So where do I recommend you put these notes or responses to the **Action Items**? Every chapter has at least one blank **NOTES** page at the end for that exact purpose. It is to provide you with a convenient place to answer your **Action Items** Questions right here in the book. This way all your notes and thoughts on this topic are together in one place for your future and easy reference.

5.   The last step in reading each chapter is to pull out your **Post-it note**™ **Tape Flags**. (I know, Finally, Huh?) Decide what the most **important topic** is for YOU in this chapter and write it across the top of a Tape Flag. This will be the index word by which you will locate the information in this chapter later.

Tape Flags with a key word written on top of the flag are a great way to identify the topic of this page and section and make it easy to come back to this specific area later. They become **your own personal index** to the book without having to rely on the table of contents or the book index (which are the author's index to the book). They are for your own handy and easy reference later when you want to find those specific pages or sections quickly

Grand March

Tape Flag
with
Key Word
Label on top

Consider - - - How will you later think of this information when you want to find it? This is the Key Word to put on the Tape Flag

6.   Now **stick your Tape Flag** on the **top of the right hand page** and you are officially finished with this chapter.

However, - - - if there happens to be more than one key idea or concept in the chapter, it is perfectly OK to use more than one Tape Flag to identify it. Now pull out a second Tape Flag, label it and stick it on the top of a page in the chapter for future reference. Then you are officially finished with the chapter.

*   *   *

In Summary those are the Bonus Tips. Now It's time to get started reading.

If you have not been to the office store yet to load your tool box with the items you need to get started, then this is your first stop. Hurry back.

If you have your tools now get your fiancé so you can do this together and let's continue preparing for the best wedding reception you can ever imagine. I'm ready. Are you?

Pour those two cups of tea or lemonade and let's get going.

This is going to be fun and exciting.

The Bubbles are only ONE of the Magnets
Drawing Everyone Out to the Dance Floor

The Bride & Groom Are Enjoying the Hottest Hits with Their Guests, Surrounded by Bubbles from the Bubbles Machine at a Wedding In Appleton, Wisconsin

Sgt Steve Preston Stays Current with
ALL of Latest Music and Dance Trends

A Group of Young Ladies Enjoying the Latest
Hits from Sgt Steve at this Wedding in
Oconomowoc, Wisconsin

* * NOTES * *

Chapter 1

Saying Thank You by Celebrating With Family and Friends

What is the real purpose of having a wedding reception? Why on earth would couples spend hundreds of their hard earned dollars just to throw an elaborate party on their special day? They could just as easily get a bunch of friends and family together at the local bar down the street to celebrate their special day. After all, it would be a whole bunch cheaper, wouldn't it? Ummm. Good thought!

Obviously, if the party was all about "YOU", you would just go throw a party down at the local tavern or night club. But, it's not just about "YOU". It's also about all your friends and family who have helped both of you get to this point in your life. Shouldn't they get a chance to celebrate with you on your special day?

What's The Purpose of Your Wedding Reception?

So I ask again: What really is the purpose of having a wedding reception? Look at it this way. This is a major milestone in both of your lives. You both have been through a lot to get here. And contrary to popular belief, you had help to get to this point. This would be as good a time as any to say Thank You!! It's what this time is all about.

So with this in mind, the answer to the question "What really is the purpose of a Wedding Reception?" becomes fairly simple to answer. And all your wedding reception planning should be reflective of this answer.

Your party is a celebration and it is not just about you. It is about your family, your guests AND you. Your family and guests are coming to the party or reception to celebrate and honor you. And in many cases, if you are fortunate to have your parents be part of your wedding, then this reception event is also partly about them. You need to make sure your family and guests are happy too. All event guests will have diverse tastes. You must consider everyone as you plan your event.

Now by no means am I saying you can't play your favorite songs or doing a dance or game the both of you enjoyed playing on your first dates. You might even have a favorite food you want on the menu. But by completely ignoring your family or guests, you are asking for a lot of trouble, not to mention family unrest for years to come. But if you can prevent this situation now, why not?

Everyone Has a Place at the Table

In many cases, the families of the bride and groom come from different backgrounds. And because of this, will have much different tastes in food, music, atmosphere, etc. This makes it doubly important you take your family and guests into consideration. It's not only the families you have to worry about; it's also the guests they want to invite as well. Always remember, your family will have a list of people they will want to invite.

A perfect example of this type of situation is where one side of the family comes from a much more affluent background than the other. I have seen this situation all too often where the side of the family which might be a little more well off takes over the wedding planning to make sure everyone knows how well off they are. This can have major consequences later, after the wedding, if not dealt with early in the process.

Allowing one side of the aisle to dominate the wedding planning can lead to resentment on both sides and can make for a complete disaster on your special day. Not only do the bride and groom need to keep family and guests in mind while planning their wedding reception, they also need to ensure both sides have a say in the planning process.

Not having both bride and groom engaged in the planning process can lead to major arguments and unwanted stress right before or (worse yet!) even **ON** your special day. I remember one wedding I did where the groom came to my office several days before the wedding to threaten me once he found out what type of entertainment his bride and her family had selected. I told the bride about it and fortunately, the bride held her ground and everybody had a wonderful time.....everybody except the groom.

When both bride and groom are engaged in the planning process, your odds increase greatly everybody will have a lot of fun on your special day and no one will feel left out regardless of social status.

Visit the Location <u>Before</u> the Day of

You also need to keep in mind some family and guests might become uncomfortable about being in a certain environment which in the end might also lead to some resentment later on. I always encourage both families to visit and dine at the reception location beforehand to make sure everyone gets the proper lay of the land prior to the day of the event. This way everyone has a chance to walk around without pressure and see the surroundings, ask questions and get comfortable. Let's say the bride and groom decides to host their reception at a local country club. For those family members and even members of the wedding party who don't spend much time at country clubs, it can be a very intimidating venue. By dining at the location (and maybe even playing tennis or golf) ahead of time you go a long way to reducing the intimidation factor and increasing the comfort level. It helps show everyone just why you and your fiancé like this place so much. Take the family there again if you need to! Why not if it helps to bridge the emotional comfort gap before the big event day, right?

It can also be viewed as a slap in the face to family members who are not as well off. This can be easily avoided by bringing members of the family and maybe even certain wedding party or key guests to the location so they become comfortable with the environment. It also serves as an excellent welcoming gesture and "getting to know you time" to the other side of the family.

This also works the other way as well if the reception is being held at a location where some family members might view as beneath them. Explain to them how this location is really where you want to hold your reception and you want to invite them to this location a couple of times so everyone can feel comfortable and no one will feel disrespected.

At the end of the day, it's about everybody having fun. No matter what the venue, your wedding entertainment should reflect the fun you want all your family and friends to have. Whether it's a Country Club or your standard banquet hall, there is no reason why you can't have a Stress-Free day and everybody can't have fun at your reception.

And always remember-It isn't just about the bride and groom having fun. It's about EVERYBODY, including friends and family, having fun. As you go through this book and as you start planning your special day, keep this simple concept in mind and your special day will go off without a hitch.

The key to preventing this from happening is asking people from the local area to help with a little research. If you're going to do something different then make sure it has some thought and planning behind it. Make it FUN then you'll be just fine.

It's when we don't think these things through completely ahead of time, and don't think of how we would feel if "the shoe were on the

Resource

Go get your own **Wedding Reception Vendor Status Checklist** to help you keep track of and organize all of your reception suppliers, along with a variety of other check lists and tips from Sgt. Steve on the Quick-Start Toolkit to help you plan your Wedding Reception in the Appendix of this book. You can also go directly to www.WeddingReceptionSecrets.com and place your order immediately!

other foot" when the trouble starts to brew. Don't let this happen to you and you will have removed one HUGE Stress-Generator.

---

* * ACTION ITEMS * *

1. Have you thought of an overall theme or vision you want to have for your wedding reception?
2. Have you thought through how everyone can participate with the theme you are considering?
3. What kind of budget are you working with for your wedding and wedding reception? _____
4. Considering your budget, how many people are you considering inviting? (Family, Friends, Friends of Parents)
5. Have you set a date to have a meal at the reception location (if possible) with your fiancé, the parents and selected members of the wedding party so everyone can get comfortable with the location?

"Steve's Vast Experience in Planning Wedding Entertainment Events Gave Us Great Confidence.

<u>No Detail Would be Overlooked!</u>"

"We just got married last Saturday (9/27/14) and Sgt. Steve Preston did an AMAZING job!!!!! He kept the dance floor full all night and made the entire night so much fun!!!!!!

We sat down with him a few weeks prior to the wedding and went through every detail and song we did and didn't want played. If we weren't sure on a song he gave us great ideas. There were so many details that my husband and I never would have though of if it wasn't for Steve and his Wedding Reception Planner Tool.

If you want our event to be a **Stress-Free night to remember** then Sgt Steve Preston and his company Sound Advice is the way to go!!!!!"

* * NOTES * *

* * NOTES * *

Chapter 2

Check the Calendar for Conflicting Events on <u>Your</u> Date

The three most important things to coordinate together on your date are the calendar for the church, banquet hall and your entertainment.

First, Get Out Your Calendar and Hurry!

Make sure you research the date you are going to book your wedding. This is the A Number One thing you have to do and the farther up front you can do it the fewer surprises you will have later on. If you are considering holding your reception event outside the geographic area where you or your fiancé reside, this is even more important. In fact, highlight this line and put some stars by it in the margin of the book if this applies to you. **<u>This is a writer downer, or since I have it written down, it's an under-liner for you!!</u>**

When you come from outside the area, you are likely not aware of the special events or even the routine normal events going on in those cities and communities where you do not live. You need to check with the chamber of commerce and the convention & visitors bureau in the location and neighboring locations to where you are planning on holding your wedding reception event to find out what is going on during the competing time frames.

These events could potentially consume all of the key banquet facilities and huge blocks of hotel rooms during the periods of time you want to hold your wedding reception event. Do your research in advance. THEN pick your dates so you do not have to compete.

If you do choose to compete with other events for dates, then just make sure you get enough hotel rooms blocked and you get your event room under a contract which cannot be cancelled under any circumstances. Consider too, what your guests will think of the higher hotel room costs during a special event period. And you too, are likely to incur additional costs and higher fees for all the services at a hotel or room venue for your reception event too.

Just ask yourself: How far do you want your budget to go? Remember if you are competing with other big events for dates, your budget will not stretch as far. Everything you want to do will cost you more. From food to entertainment to your guest's hotel rooms, you can expect to pay from 10% to 100% more than on an off weekend. It's your decision.

Steve's Sound Advice

The "A" Number #1 Thing To Do Is Pick Your Date And Two Alternates

You can never start too early to lock down the important venue and date for your reception.

I remember one couple who decided on their wedding date and found out later it was Harley Davidson's 110th Anniversary and when it came time to reserve a block of hotel rooms for the wedding party and some guests, they couldn't get any rooms. Everything was already booked. When deciding on your date, do a simple Google search on both the date and area of your event. One of the most common mistakes couples make when booking their wedding date is not being aware of what else is going on in the area around their preferred date. Do a little research, and do it early. Be a wary shopper here and you can save your guests a lot of money and especially a lot of hassle.

When I was planning my wedding, it was going to be during the following year's Experimental Aircraft Association Convention in Oshkosh, WI. It is one of the biggest events each year in Northeast WI. However, since we knew it was coming up, we booked a block of rooms, for our guests over a year in advance. As long as you do the research and homework up front, in advance, you should be okay.

So, as you learned in school do your homework, do your research. You don't want to end up with bad results. Don't be lazy. It's a matter of simple preparation. Keep in mind - - this is your day and it's supposed to be fun. The Ultimate Forget Me Knot Wedding Planner™ is there for you to make sure you take care of everything in advance. The plan will result in a fun, Stress-Free and successful event.

* * ACTION ITEMS * *

1. Get your calendar out and discuss your ideal date. Select TWO alternate dates.
2. Use all possible means to research conflicting events with your ideal date in the geographic vicinity of your reception. (If a conflict is found, repeat steps for alternate dates).
3. If no conflicts are found, make sure your church, reception location and your DJ Entertainer have all firmed up your ideal date on **their** calendars by signing **each** one of their contracts.

Sgt Steve Delivers On His Promises No Matter What The Event

I recently hired Sgt. Steve Preston's Sound Advice for my husband's 40th surprise birthday party. I knew Steve booked for a variety of events, but was pleasantly surprised at how perfect he was even for our particular party. Not only was I impressed and happy with his ideas, coordination and the music he helped me select, but also with every announcement Steve provided during the evening. Some of our guests made sure to tell us what a great DJ Steve was. Our party was a tremendous success in large part because Steve set and carried the tone every minute of the evening. Steve inquired about and honored every one my special requests, and was very accommodating. I have no doubt anyone looking for music and a real professional DJ will be extremely satisfied with Sgt. Steve Preston Zuelzke's Sound Advice.

Sara Bodensteiner- Brown-2015

* * NOTES * *

Chapter 3

Select the Proper Venue –
It's a Balancing Act

How Well Can You Juggle ......?

So you have now narrowed down the date of the big day on the calendar and now it's time to start talking numbers. Hopefully this will not be the first time you both have had a discussion about how much you want to invest in your big day. And of course you'll want to invite everyone!! – Everyone does at first. Then we need to get realistic and do a review of the budget!

And if you are both fortunate enough to have parents in the picture, they too will have a whole host of friends who they will want to invite. After all, they are proud of both of you and want to show you off on your big day. As all brides and grooms quickly find out, this is where the juggling act begins.

You just can't invite everyone, - - - Unless - - - you don't care about having entertainment, cake, flowers, etc.

This is where the balancing/juggling act begins between the cost of feeding your guests, the size of the banquet hall you need (or can afford) and who you want to invite. It is how well you balance these three factors and then how accurately you can predict who will actually show up at the event and now you can relieve one of the biggest stress factors on your wedding day.

Most People Start With the Budget and I Recommend You Start There Too

Figuring out how much you want to spend will greatly influence how many people you can realistically invite. And in turn it will effect where it will make sense to hold your wedding reception too. I suggest by starting here, and balancing these factors, and you'll be surprised just how much you'll still be able to invest in top quality and experienced DJ Entertainment.

Steve's Sound Advice

Don't Get Caught Overspending On Less Important Items Or You Won't Have Budget Left For The Things Which Mean The Most To You In The End

(Yes, my bias does show through here – **I believe there are a** whole host of reasons why a top notch DJ Entertainer is the best value over any other type of entertainment you can choose. – I will have more on why I believe this to be the case in a succeeding chapter. Stay tuned.)

The Guest List – Ohhh, Does Size Matter!!

This takes us to the question of whether you are going to use a banquet facility which will also supply your food. If the answer is yes, then you automatically answer another question about the charge for the banquet facility because it is built into the food cost. This makes your budgeting much easier.

If, on the other hand, you will still have the ability to cater in food from the outside at a hall you choose, then there will likely be a separate line item charge to use the hall. Remember to budget for the hall separately.

This will in turn guide you to a menu of food choices, which will each have their own per person cost. From here you can back into how many guests you can afford to feed based on your reception budget.

Based on what you would like to serve, you know a per plate cost. Then this per plate cost divided into your total reception budget results in how many guests you can afford to feed. This will result in a total number of guests you can afford to invite. Remember this first calculation includes all the no-shows too.

This now will help you set the budget for everything else going forward. Here is also where a lot of difficult and honest discussions have to take place. In most weddings, the bride and groom and the parents discuss and reach agreement on a fair number of guests for each of them to invite. The sum of each will total up to the total budget number.

Unless you have an unlimited budget, you are not going to be able to invite everyone. And if you remember back in Chapter 1, your parents need to participate in this key discussion. (**Remember, it's not all about you!!**)

Spend too much of your budget here and you got big trouble later on.

Also keep the following statistic in mind when discussing just how large the guest list will be. According to "The Knot", a well-known wedding publication, only 75 to 80% of invited guests will actually show up. So obviously, not everybody you invite will attend for some reason or another. For example, if you invite 100 guests to your wedding, you can expect 75-80 to attend.

But does it mean only 75-80% attend every time? Of course not. Using this example, the bride and groom might just go ahead and budget for 80 and hope the other 20 don't come. If you hit the 80 or less number, you're golden. If 90-100 actually attend; you run over budget (maybe run out of food) and get an unpleasant surprise at the end of the night.

Knowing this, here is a really good rule of thumb no matter how big your guest list. Always budget for 20-25% more guests than the actual number you decided on. For example, if you invite 100 people then plan to pay for 120-125 people. This will not only cover you if all 100 people do happen to show up, but you will also be covered in the event of any last minute additions or friends and family your parents may have forgotten to tell you about. (Or children who were brought along by parents who did not RSVP for them.)

If you can't afford to budget for 20-25 more than your original list, then your original list will have to shrink to where you can afford a little margin. Not taking this into account in your planning will just lead to a lot of needless and anxious stress later on.

Always remember, your entire wedding budget isn't just for dinner. It's for everything! Overspending in this area will lead to having to cut back in other areas.

How Would You FEEL If You Were Getting Compliments Like These About the DJ Entertainer at Your Wedding Reception? . . .
You Can FEEL Exactly the Same
When You Select . . .
. . . Sgt Steve Preston Zuelzke for YOUR Reception

Dear Steve,

We cannot **thank you enough** for the superb service you provided us! You are definitely a DJ who **OVER delivers** on every aspect we agreed on. Thank you for meeting with us, previewing our venue site and providing such great energy for our event. **We received so many compliments** about your great music choices and the bubbles were a huge hit. **Everything went so smoothly. You deserve to be paid MUCH more.** You were the gem of all our wedding vendors!!! You truly were the shining star of our event!!!

Thank You,
The Burwells

Size (Room) Does Matter....

Once you have cut the wedding invite list to a number you are both comfortable with, it's time to do the balancing with a venue (assuming you don't already have one which will accommodate any number you invite). The venue must be able to comfortably hold the number of guests you are inviting and if it is going to be a separate line item charge, when you add their fee in, also be within your budget.

Knowing the number of guests you are planning to invite when walking into a meeting with banquet hall owners and hotel sales managers can give you an advantage and keep stress levels low. It will allow you to quickly assess whether or not the maximum number of guests in a particular layout works for the number you are inviting. It will also prevent you from getting sold on a venue too large for what you need but makes the owner more money.

Doing your numbers ahead of time will save you money, guaranteed! More importantly however ending up with a room way too big for your reception will absolutely

> # Resource
>
> Go get your own **Venue Assessment Guide** to help you evaluate each venue, along with a variety of other check lists and tips from Sgt. Steve on the Quick-Start Toolkit to help you plan your Wedding Reception in the Appendix of this book. You can also go directly to www.WeddingReceptionSecrets.com and place your order immediately

kill the ambience of the party. Nothing sucks the

life out of a room faster than the feeling of a mostly empty room.

Lately, in recent years, many wedding dinner receptions have gotten smaller. The average wedding size today is about 100 to 150 people. This leaves a ton of huge banquet halls to choose from for your wedding event in almost every city across the country. If you are hosting only a hundred people into a hall with a maximum capacity of 500 or more, you need to think about how this is going to look on your evening and later in your pictures.

How Do You Know How Many Guests To Invite?
Sample Calculation

(In This Example the Banquet Room Fee
is Included in the Food Cost

Reception Budget	$6,000.00
Dinner Item Cost ++ Per Plate	$25.00
Number who RSVP "No"	15%
Number who RSVP "Yes" but we estimate will be a "NO Show" the day of	20%
Number we will budget "Over" for	10%

1. Start by: $6,000 divided by $25 = 240 Max guests your budget allows. This is the pre-RSVP NO factor
2. Subtract 15%, so 240 x 85% = 204
3. Then 204 x 80% = 163, this is the number resulting after you account for No Shows at the door
4. Lastly add back 10% so 163 + 10% = 180
5. Add family and wedding party to this number, if they are not already taken into account to get a grand total

Conclusions-

1. Your budget allows for 240 Maximum guests (remember to include members of your wedding party and family!)
2. Using your estimates, when inviting 240 guests, will result in 180 people at the reception
3. You need to test – Is this number OK for the size hall you are planning to use
4. Can you invite more guests, less guests?
5. Here is where your balancing begins

WORKSHEET

How Many Guests Can YOU Invite to YOUR Reception?
(In This Example the Banquet Room Fee
is Included in the Food Cost

Fill in YOUR Numbers Here to Practice

Reception Budget $\qquad$ \$_____ (A)

Dinner Item Cost ++ Per Plate \$_____ (B)

% who RSVP "No" _____% (C)

% who RSVP "Yes" but we estimate

  will be a "NO Show" the day of _____% (D)

% Surprise guests we will budget "Over" for _____% (E)

1. A divided by B = F _____ (Max Guest Pre RSVP)
2. F times (100-C%) =G _____ (Number after RSVP)
3. G times (100-D%)=H _____ (Num after No Show)
4. H times (100+E%)=J _____ (Num after Surprise
   Guests showing up the day of the event)
5. J equals your starting number.
6. J Plus family Plus wedding party = K
7. How does K compare to your venue capacity?

Conclusions-
1. If your venue capacity is larger than K, then you can feel comfortable inviting more guests.
2. Plug a larger number into F and repeat your calculations until your resulting number at K is the maximum you are comfortable with.

The big take away here is very few couples have an unlimited budget to spend on their wedding and reception, so sticking to your budget is very important. But even the most budget conscious couples are susceptible to spending way too much when they don't need to and spending less when they could be inviting a few more special guests and friends. Know your numbers and this won't be you!!

* * **ACTION ITEMS** * *

1. How many people does your budget allow you to host?
2. Have you used the sample calculation in this chapter to determine the max number to invite?
3. Can you afford and do you have a banquet room which can handle 120% of this number in case this maximum number actually shows up?
4. Once you have identified a location for your reception, Identify who the point of contact is going to be for your evening and make sure he/she is someone you can easily work with.

Sgt Steve Makes Weddings Much More Fun by
Getting Everyone Out Onto the Dance Floor
with Fun, Unique, and Interactive Dances Sure to
Please Everyone!!

At this Appleton, Wisconsin Wedding The Dance Floor
Remained Full All Night Long!

* * NOTES * *

Chapter 4

Compare Your Entertainment Options

In spite of the fact this book is authored by a DJ Entertainer, and one of the best I might add too, it is important to point out you actually have several viable entertainment options for your wedding reception event.

Let's look at the pluses and the minuses here. Far and above the most popular, in order, are:

1. DJ Entertainers
2. Cover Band
3. VJ (a video disc jockey) and
4. Karaoke.

A DJ Entertainer, Who Serves As the <u>Master Of Ceremonies</u> <u>For The Evening</u>, Is <u>Always A Much Better Fit</u> Than Simply Hiring A Band

Steve,
We just wanted to say Thank You for the excellent job you did for us at our wedding. **We received so many complements about you**, especially the bubble machines.

We would recommend you to anyone. A DJ can definitely make or break a wedding and you definitely made our night perfect and complete in every way.

Thanks Again,
Julie and Dennis

I am going to present the DJ Entertainer option in more detail in the next chapter. Let's explore each of the other options here in this chapter.

Let's First Inspect Cover Bands:

The Positives:

The first HUGE positive is it's a live band. Most people like live bands. No. Let me restate this. Most people LOVE live bands. Folks like to see the artistry of others performing and playing their instruments. Most people like to see themselves up there performing and playing one of those instruments live like one of those good performers. Many of us have a secret rock or live performer side who we wish we could have emulated and been as good as many years ago. As such, we love to see some special instrument being played live whenever we can. A live band will out-draw a DJ every time if this were the only difference. Now I hope folks are not making a decision whether to attend your wedding based on the entertainment you are providing but you get the picture. Getting close to a live band is a HUGE draw if we were talking about a concert setting only.

The Negatives:

It is well known how too often the bad reputation of a band precedes them. They are notorious for their wild, sometimes bad-mannered and oftentimes unprofessional behavior. Now we hope when you select a specific cover band for your wedding reception event, much of the "reputation risk" has already been vetted out by others, but you always have some of this type of risk.

With any cover band, beginning with the contracting process, you are usually dealing with several levels of people, including a talent agency, not just one contact. Each of them comes with an ego needing soothing.

Cover Bands, whose individual members also have big egos, also have a reputation and real problems of staying together for too long because they need to have their egos fed too. When a member feels their ego is being bruised, they leave the band and go to another band or even go off to start their own band.

So by choosing a cover band many months in advance of your event (which is absolutely the right thing to do) you are running the risk of not seeing the same band members who you signed up many months back.

I receive calls periodically from brides and grooms as well as event organizers in a panic pleading with me, "Steve, please, please help me. I need a big favor. (As if this were the first time they were asking!) The band I hired is no longer even playing together. They have a different name. They have different members. I can't trust their music anymore. I now want you. (With Panic in their squeaky voice) Do you have a particular date and time available? Can you **Please** help me? . . . *Please!*"

Most cover bands don't know how to do weddings. What I mean is they know how to play music very well but music is where it ends. They are excellent musicians, without a wedding specialty. They haven't been together long enough and have never been trained in the special techniques to bring a wedding together and allow, for instance, the photographer to get those special memory pictures at the special times during a wedding. For instance, without your (the bride or groom's) coaching, guidance and insistence, there will be no dinner/cocktail music and no one will know to do the announcements of the Grand Entrances or Grand March. They often take breaks, at inopportune times and struggle with adjusting to or even playing the music the crowd wants and needs. The leader of the band is not adept at coordinating a wedding as a DJ Entertainer is at being the Master of Ceremonies of your wedding reception.

Steve's Sound Advice

Most People Think Entertainment First But Remember You Are Also Selecting Your Master Of Ceremonies For The Evening

Most cover bands remind me of the movie "The Blues Brothers," especially the scene where they get booked into a country western bar and play Rawhide all night long, over and over and over again.

I'm not saying there are no good wedding cover bands, but they are few and far between. Again it comes down to your taste. This is a good place for me to remind you how important it is to do a live a comparison of the cover band and the DJ entertainer you are considering for your event. This is where you want to see both of them in action (**doing a wedding reception**) before you pick one for your event. Your eyes and ears will help you make your decision here.

Do you recall what the one big item is? It is the ultimate crowd killer. They take breaks. In fact it's actually how the DJ entertainment industry got started. Did you know back in the late 70's and early 80's I and a lot of other DJ's were hired to play for bands while they took their breaks. Anytime the band turned out to be bad or even somewhat mediocre, (which was most of the time) they would be sent packing and the DJ would take over as the entertainment for the rest of the night. I can't emphasize enough how DJ entertainment is both the flexibility and the expertise to truly make your event a HUGE success.

Another Entertainment Alternative Is the (Video DJ) Entertainer.

The Video DJ is also called a VJ for short. This person tries to be both a DJ entertainer and a VJ.

The Positives:

The big positive attribute of a VJ entertainer is the participants can actually SEE the video of the artist performing the music at the time during your event. It's almost like attending a concert. And let's be honest. Folks like attending concerts.

In this world of music videos on television and in the theaters and on their iPods, etc., seeing the videos at wedding events is just an extension of what they are already used to. People like Music Videos and you don't have to actually dance to fully enjoy the video either.

One can be an idle bystander and still have a good time, however, when you think about it, this is probably not the conducive for a wedding reception where you really want the focus to be on the dance floor or on the bride and groom.

The Negatives:

On the other hand, the downside or negatives of hiring a VJ is the challenge of creating an interactive crowd. The biggest difficulty here starts with the lighting. In order to effectively see the videos on large television screens, the room lighting is dim or at a minimum much lower. (It

interferes with the TV screens.) In addition most of the sound quality is TV quality which is much less than band or DJ quality. People get mesmerized by watching the videos. They get used to NOT dancing and just sitting in their chairs, drinking and chatting. It is very difficult to instigate a dancing interactive atmosphere when videos are playing on the big screens.

Another Alternative Is Karaoke.

The Positives:

In this instance, the coordinator acts like a DJ or the star singer. Your family and guests get to be the stars. They each can sing their favorite songs, alone and with each other. This format breeds a lot of fun, joking around and having fun with the other guests.

The Negatives:

The downside or negatives of a karaoke event are all of the breaks in the music. No music is played while the karaoke person is trying to get Uncle Bob to the stage. Now you've just killed the momentum of the event. In addition, you're going to hear some poor or even lousy singers, people you can't stand. You are also bound to hear Uncle George's twenty renditions of Elvis. Some people get sick of karaoke and want to dance. Sometimes without the dancing, you lose the feel and flow of the wedding night and the remaining guests get bored and will start to leave. Karaoke is not a very popular form of

wedding reception entertainment these days unless one is really trying to manage the budget to a minimum.

One Other Wedding Reception Entertainment Idea

Did you ever consider a polka band? I bring this up because I'm from the Midwest where seeing a polka band at a wedding reception in the 50's 60's and 70's was as common as seeing raw beef, sliced onions and rye bread on the serving table. A lot has changed since then.

The Positives:

If you decide to hire a polka band, you will certainly appeal to the older set. Your grandparents will love you for it. As we have said before, the followers of the live band will also be enamored by the folks playing live instruments. There is always an attraction to live bands.

The Negatives:

The crowd will tire of the band quickly due to the narrowness of their music variety. Especially the younger crowd - - - They will be bored most quickly. A polka band's problem is the same as a cover band. As the night goes on the crowd is going to be looking for some new top 40 hits, dance and classic rock music. These are music varieties a polka band usually cannot deliver.

As with any other band, without your (the bride or groom's) coaching, guidance and insistence, there will likely be no dinner/cocktail music and no one will know to do the special wedding reception announcements like the Grand Entrances or Grand March. They often take breaks at inopportune times and struggle with adjusting to or even playing the music the crowd wants and needs. The leader of the band is not adept at coordinating a wedding as a DJ Entertainer is at being the Master of Ceremonies of your wedding reception.

Just try to imagine your favorite polka band trying to do Katy Perry, Usher, Lynyrd Skynyrd or Nickelback! Yes, Hard to imagine! I agree!

If you survey the banquet facilities about what is the best and most versatile entertainment option, they will agree with me, hire a good professional DJ entertainer, and you have a winner every time.

You should try to match the entertainer to the crowd you're inviting. My personal suggestion to you is to look very seriously at the DJ entertainment option. It is the option who has the best chance of making your event a rousing success. The next chapter will explain exactly why in detail.

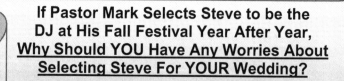

If Pastor Mark Selects Steve to be the DJ at His Fall Festival Year After Year, <u>Why Should YOU Have Any Worries About Selecting Steve For YOUR Wedding?</u>

I just wanted to Thank You for once again providing your outstanding DJ service for our Fall Festival at Faith Lutheran Church. I attend many wedding receptions as a Lutheran minister, and rarely do I experience as Professional a Performance as you provide for us each year.

You are most welcome to use my name as a recommendation or reference for future business contacts. I would not hesitate to recommend Sound Advice for any occasion.

Blessings,
Mark Abram, Pastor

A Couple Last Red Flags (From Experience)

A note on communications -

Some entertainment services won't even talk to you on the phone. They'll communicate with you through email or Facebook only. To my way of thinking this is **a huge red flag**. You need to ask Why? On the other hand you may be comfortable communicating this way but please beware, it is still a BIG RED FLAG in my book.

Are they returning your calls or responding to your emails in a timely fashion? If not, **another red flag**. If you give him/her instructions, do they follow those instructions? If not, then **another red flag**. At this point, two or more Red Flags mean contact another entertainment service. You can't just keep accumulating Red Flags!!

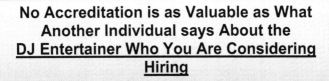

No Accreditation is as Valuable as What Another Individual says About the DJ Entertainer Who You Are Considering Hiring

Steve-
We want to thank you for the terrific DJ job you did at our wedding. Many people complimented us on the music you played and how you kept the crowd dancing. You even had Myron out on the floor dancing-And Myron Never Dances!!
Thank you also for recording the music during the reception. The recordings will be a nice remembrance of the good time we had at our reception. We will definitely recommend you to everyone!!

Thanks Again,
Stacy and Tom

A note on Banquet Hall Owners who seems too pushy - Beware of the banquet hall manager who is always pushing for one cover band or one particular DJ. Sometime when you ask a banquet manager's opinion, you are going to get the same old answer. Some hall managers are going to be biased because they are receiving some type of perks from certain vendor companies.

Resource

Remember to use the
DJ Assessment in Chapter 17
to help you make the best choice for your DJ Entertainer.
This Assessment is also provided to you in electronic form in the Toolkit.
By going to
www.WeddingReceptionSecrets.com

* * ACTION ITEMS * *

1. Decide on which entertainment option you want. Ask yourself why you picked a different option other than a DJ entertainer

2. If you picked a cover band for your entertainment, have you checked them out carefully to insure the band you thought you hired is the one that will show up on the day of your reception? Is it all in writing?

3. If you have elected to have a VJ or karaoke based wedding, will there be someone there to man the equipment during your reception to ensure it remains up and running for you?

Steve Has a Very Special Talent You Won't Find Anywhere Else of Entertaining All Age Groups. He Magnetically Attracts Everyone Out Dancing He Helped Everyone Feel Upbeat All Night Long!!

Sgt. Steve Preston-
Thank You for making our wedding day a true success!
You certainly kept everyone dancing and feeling upbeat. I
absolutely enjoyed every minute of the reception! (My feet
STILL ACHE!!). It was very thoughtful of you to record the
reception music. We will cherish that gift for many years to
come!

Thanks Again and Keep Rockin!!
Jill and Brian

Steve Was Thorough in Conducting and Managing Our Day

Steve,
We wanted to thank you for doing such a great job at our
wedding. Everyone still tells us how much fun they had
and how great you were. All other wedding and DJ's pale
in comparison! You really are amazing at what you do
and our wedding would not have been the same without
you as our DJ.

Thanks Again,
Brian and Kristy

P.S. Thank you for the recordings. We never expected
that and we listened to them over and over again on our
honeymoon!

* * NOTES * *

Chapter 5

Accept Only the Best for Your Wedding Entertainment *(You Deserve It!)*

❝ *The Appleton Post-Crescent interviewed me a few years ago about my views on the local entertainment industry. The newspaper reporter told me they were doing an article on the DJ Entertainment business and he was contacting me because of my longevity in the industry. The interview consisted of a collection of some rather basic questions and I thought the interview went really well. I thought I had done a good job of explaining the modern positioning of the DJ Entertainer in today's business environment.* **❞**

A few weeks later, however, when the article was published, my jaw dropped. I realized then, one of my competitors had also been interviewed. In my comments, I had taken the high road and positioned the DJ Entertainment Industry in the professional light it deserved. Much to my total surprise, this competitor, had sabotaged everything I said. His comments were something to the effect - - -

*"All DJ's do is just **make a lot of noise** . . . and he could **train a monkey** to do what DJ's do and his staff of monkeys could make money this way."*

Allow me in the rest of this chapter to demonstrate the total foolishness in the above thought.

The Environment
Your DJ Entertainer Creates For You
Is the Lifeline of Your Event

The environment truly has the ability to make or break your party and make or break your entire afternoon or evening. No matter what type of entertainment you choose, if it turns out not to be good, or not well received, then your party is going to be pretty much over — and it's going to be over much earlier than you want.

Why? Because in spite of the fact many of your guests are your closest friends, they will quietly start heading for the exits, often without saying a word because they do not want to embarrass you or hurt your feelings. The only sign you will see is the dance floor and the ballroom will start to look very empty.

You Will Wonder, "What Happened?"

If you follow the guidelines in this "How-to" book, you will have a fun and Stress-Free event. More importantly, you will be able to budget for and afford an outstanding and experienced DJ Entertainer to create a fantastic and most memorable experience for you and your fiancé. – **I Guarantee It.**

Sgt Steve Preston Zuelcke

I am designing this book to help you understand you don't have to settle for the **CHEAPEST** or the **LEAST** when it comes to hiring DJ entertainment. You should never hire a DJ Entertainer where you need to tell him/her how to handle every minute of the time he/she spends entertaining your guests. A good analogy is you never have to tell a restaurant chef what the menu should be or tell the kitchen staff how to properly cook a meal when you go to a fine place to dine.

After all, this IS what you are looking for, isn't it? This is all part of my promise to you.

There is a common myth or stereotype of a specific type of DJ. The industry calls him/her the 'YO DJ' person.

Steve Took the Time to Get to Know Us So Well <u>Before</u> the Event <u>It Felt Like He Was Part of my Family</u>

Steve,
Thank you so much for the excellent DJ service for my party. You were excellent and we got a lot of compliments on you. Everyone thought you were related because you knew what we liked. You will always be recommended by us.

Thanks Again,
LeRoy, Colleen, and Sara

They are the type of person who:

♦ Doesn't care what they look like
♦ Wears inappropriate clothing
♦ Wears a ball cap backwards (quite often)
♦ Thinks they are the coolest (whatever that means at the time)

- Still uses vinyl records
- Never uses the microphone (even when one is there)
- Mixes only newer rap, dance or R&B music and
- Scratches the vinyl records with a wicka, wicka, wicka sound. (on purpose)

I am careful to refer to this person as a stereotype because magazines, television and the movies use this type of 'YO DJ' person all the time whenever they need to portray a DJ type person. This is a very sad situation. It's sad because the majority of DJs in this country are not like this at all. They are NOT the 'YO DJ' person I described above. The majority of DJ's do NOT fit the stereotype.

Steve's Sound Advice

You Will Be Shocked How Much DJ Entertainer You Can Afford When You Manage Your Budget Correctly

The Goal: What the Industry Calls a Professional DJ Entertainer

It is the **Professional DJ Entertainer** title which much more fully describes the real job we do and the functions we provide at an event. In fact, we are actually much more entertainers than DJ's. We are in so many cases the glue holding your event together when the unexpected happens.

A good DJ entertainer is a person who does live events on a regular basis, relies on it for a living and not just as a part-time hobby.

©2015 Sound Advice Music and Entertainment

Here is how to think of it. In fact, I recommend you write the following on a 3 x 5 Index Card or Post-It note and put in on your mirror if you have not selected a DJ Entertainer for your wedding reception yet. It will serve as a good Goal for you.

The **DJ Entertainer** I am hiring is my

"Behind The Scenes Master Of Ceremonies"

and my stage manager for the reception event! This is the person who is carrying out my wishes and coordinating the evening's activities while my fiancé and I are having the time of our life with family, friends and guests.

© 2015 Sound Advice Music and Entertainment

Consider, Ummmmm - - - - - Do you want to be worrying about every little step, every little agenda item, every little timing of every activity and being concerned if it is going to be carried out as you had discussed when you laid out the agenda several weeks before - - - - - or do you want to be enjoying the evening and partying with all your family, friends and guests creating memories of a lifetime? I think I know your answer. You want to be in "enjoyment mode," right?

But how do you get to this point? You don't want to be thinking about the details once your special day starts. You want to have all the wedding reception event planning done.

Let's look in more detail here about what your expectations should be for the professional DJ Entertainer you hire for your wedding reception event. How do I know? Easy. This is what I do. So I have a little inside information here for you. This is also why just anyone cannot write this book like I can.

Please take advantage of this inside information. What I am saying is: *"Select a DJ Entertainer who has these things in their brochure and lives up to them when you see them live."* This should be part of <u>the "standard" you are setting</u> for the person you select. This is by no means too much to expect. **It is possible!**

And besides - - - - you deserve it! - Don't let anyone try to tell you it is necessary to accept any

less, or to suggest this level of quality does not exist. **Because This Level of Quality DOES EXIST!**

Your DJ Entertainer will:
Be **Ready** before you are by:

1. Being Punctual to all meetings, especially the big day itself
2. Having everything set up way before the event starts
3. When you work with a professional DJ, you get who you are meeting with and speaking to each step of the way. No substitutes or last minute lineup changes (like could happen with a band)

Your DJ Entertainer will:
Demonstrate their deep **Experience by:**

1. Caring about every detail
2. Dressing appropriately (as you requested)
3. Never being afraid of the microphone
4. Doing their very best to keep the dance floor busy all evening
5. Focusing totally on making the bride & groom be the stars of the evening – not on them, not on the music or on anything else
6. Giving the people what they want.
7. Driving the crowd
8. Maintaining a Stress-Free reception environment for the bride and groom

9. Remaining mindful everything might not go as planned so be ready to adjust as necessary
10. Having done a wide variety of Wedding Receptions and Wedding Parties. (Most bands do mostly bars and public performances)
11. Serving as the M.C. (Master of Ceremonies), in many cases without the crowd even knowing he/she is the MC, they do it so smoothly
12. Being able to adjust to the direction of the crowd instantly
13. Creating a flow
14. Staying prepared to do whatever is necessary to keep the events of the evening flowing smoothly for everyone
15. **Never takes a break** – You read it right – Never!

Your DJ Entertainer will:

Show their ability to **Plan a Total Event** by:

1. Meeting before the event to set the timeline for the entire afternoon or evening
2. Executing the reception script as was agreed to weeks before at The Ultimate Wedding Review™
3. Getting the wedding party and family involved at all the right points of the event

Your DJ Entertainer will:

Demonstrate **Knowledge of Current Music** by:

1. Playing the latest music and hits and only the hits

2. Honoring the "Do not play" and "play" lists
3. Providing ceremony music no matter the location
4. Providing Dinner/Cocktail music, without blowing people out of the room
5. Offering up a variety of music. (A DJ can change Genre of music instantly)
6. Avoiding cookie cutter songs and performances
7. Playing only clean versions of music
8. Maintaining appropriate volume levels all evening
9. Resisting any temptation to "promote and play the new song I just wrote" on Joe Schmuckatelly CD's and downloads ready for you to buy today
10. Having access to the in-demand novelty songs (Hokey-Pokey, Chicken Dance, Conga line etc.)
11. Playing the type of music the crowd wants
12. Handling requests if bride/groom so chooses
13. Refusing requests politely if those are the wishes of the bride/groom

Your DJ Entertainer will:

Utilize **Current Equipment** By:

1. Demonstrating Excellent and up-to-date Sound. Let your ear answer this question for you
2. Using visually appealing and up-to-date lighting
3. Providing lighting "for the crowd" and even changing it for every song to create a changing atmosphere if warranted (A band normally has lighting only on themselves)
4. Having Back up equipment readily available in case something breaks or burns out

And Yes, There Are Still Just Regular DJ's.

You will find regular DJs working the club circuit and for the most part they are just playing song after song after song all evening long in a club or lounge environment. Their concern is what time do I start and what time do I end. This is not who you are looking to hire for your wedding reception event. You can usually cull out this type of DJ pretty quickly by asking where they do most of their work. Be polite but quickly go on to the next interview.

For One of Andy and Melanie's Guests Seeing Really Was Believing and Convincing

Steve,
Thank You very much for your high quality entertainment at our wedding!! Our Guests really had a lot of fun-and one of our engaged guests is already hiring you for her wedding!

We really appreciate your professionalism, enthusiasm, and organization in making our reception extremely enjoyable for us and our guests.

Thanks Again,
Andy and Melanie

It's Time to Make Your Hiring Decision

Conclusion: In case it is not totally clear by now, allow me to help you to conclude (without putting too many words in your mouth.) However, since I am the author of this book I am going to help you just a wee bit. Just to make sure we get it right. Here is the moral of the story -

It Pays to Review Your Prospective DJ Before You Hire Them

Dear Steve,
Thanks a ton for the fun wedding with lots of bubbles. We did our homework on the DJ and it paid off tremendously. We definitely will refer you to friends and family. You did an awesome job!!! You Rock!!!

God Bless,
Haley and Martin

If you want to have the Most **Stress-Free Wedding Reception** possible, then I want to suggest strongly the **best value you are going to get**, for every ounce of energy you put into your planning and organizing is going to be with a **Professional DJ Entertainer**. This is your best ROI, bar none!!

The way you begin is back in chapter 3. Right there you start by balancing the number of guests with the size venue, and with food costs to ensure you preserved the budget for your DJ Entertainer. When you start there, everyone will win. I promise. If you have any questions throughout this process, there is a "contact me" form on the last page of this book. Feel free to use it.

So – Hire the right person and you will have no worries!

* * ACTION ITEMS * *

1. Have you completed the DJ Assessment in Chapter 17 for each potential DJ you are considering? This is the ONLY way to insure you are selecting the BEST DJ Entertainer for your reception.
2. Review your budget to insure you are maximizing the amount you can invest in Quality Entertainment, which is what your guests will remember most.

Your DJ Entertainer. . .Sgt Steve Preston—
Your Master of Ceremonies and
Your Bride and Groom's
Director of Stress-Reduction for the Evening

Sgt Steve Preston Ready for Action,
Here in Green Bay, Wisconsin

* * NOTES * *

Chapter 6

Budget for the Right Entertainment – The Plan Starts with the Right Numbers

You will hear from all of your vendors and they will each tell you they are the most important component of your event! - - - There is some truth to what they are saying but only to a point. Let me explain here.

What is truly the most important aspect of your event? It is your entertainment. Here is one area where there are good statistics to validate the position. Let's look at them.

First ask yourself, "When YOU last attended a wedding what do you remember most?" Examiner.Com referenced an August 2011 poll from Modern Bride Magazine. In it they asked guests what they remembered most from the last wedding they attended in person. What do you suppose their answer was?

The result was: The number one thing the average wedding guest remembered was **the entertainment!** The number two thing they recalled was the **wedding dress!** The third was the **food/venue**, and fourth was the **flowers and décor**.

Conclusion: Focus on the Big Stuff. . .
. . . The Entertainment!

So what obvious conclusion would we draw from this survey of wedding guests.

Simple and NO DOUBT – **"It's the Entertainment!!"**

So . . . if you want to have a memorable wedding reception, then don't make the common mistake of spending way too much money on the venue/food, flowers, and décor because your guests are not remembering those details. Focus on your entertainment for the event. Get this part right for your guests. Make it match who the guests are in age and what kind of music and entertainment they like to hear and be around. This is what they will be talking about later, not the flowers.

Steve's Sound Advice

By Knowing And Being Firm With Your Budget When Negotiating With Entertainment, You Will Be Assured Of Getting The Very Best Possible For Your Wedding Reception

In another section of the same magazine, this same poll revealed how in reflecting on their big day, the brides and grooms polled said they regretted pinching pennies and discounting the role of their entertainment. The brides and grooms did not realize the really important role entertainment plays during the day. As a result, they did not invest enough time looking for the entertainment to do the best job and they did not invest the appropriate amount of their budget to hire the best one to support them during their reception.

In essence, they shortchanged themselves. They thought they were saving money, when in reality they were costing themselves dollars of sanity and dollars of Stress-Free'ness of their evening. Get it?

They went on to explain how they would have made it a much higher priority as they went about planning their big day.

CAUTION – Save yourself a whole lot of Money!! -- Don't error the same way yourself. Use this as a lesson you don't have to live it out in person in order to learn it.

I hear this myself time and time again. Some of the feedback I often receive when someone hires me is, "We are hiring you Steve, because I don't want my special day to turn out like one of my relatives did or one of my best friend's turned out or like my sorority sisters did.

The DJ:

- Sat in a chair
- Played slow music

♦ Played old music
♦ Looked like he did not care to be there.

The result was:

♦ Hardly anyone danced
♦ Lots of folks were bored and
♦ We all left an hour or so after they started.

Lesson – If **YOUR DJ** is into the music, **YOUR CROWD** will be into the music and react in kind too.

Remember, your DJ is your behind the scenes master of ceremonies and your stage manager for your event all night long. It is your Key position in your group. Hire Wisely!!!

What sickens me is how the lazy DJ seems to be becoming the industry norm. What is happening to the exception, good memorable entertainment? When people attend weddings or events they seem to be going ready to be expecting bad entertainment. This is terrible. It is not right. It has to stop!!

It is up to you to:
Stop Putting Up With Poor Performances
anymore! With the help of this book, I hope you can help make it stop! We are conditioning our audiences incorrectly. And remember back to the last chapter – You deserve only the BEST.

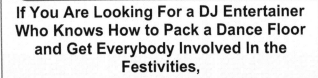

If You Are Looking For a DJ Entertainer Who Knows How to Pack a Dance Floor and Get Everybody Involved In the Festivities,

Then <u>Sgt Steve IS THE GUY You Want To Pick For Your Event</u>

We had such a great experience with Sgt. Steve! We met with him in advance and he goes over every detail to make sure your night will be exactly how YOU want it to be.

He was very good about checking in throughout the night to make sure everything was how we were expecting. Were we ready for the grand march, are there any songs we wanted to hear before the night was over that we hadn't yet, etc.

He did an ice breaker after the first dances (which we agreed to in our pre-planning meeting) which packed the dance floor and it stayed that way all night. He really knows how to cater to the crowd. He played a good variety and kept everyone dancing all night long!

I received so many compliments after the wedding of how much fun everyone had. They had never seen so many people dancing all night. I even had one person tell me that they have been to A LOT of weddings and this was the best DJ they had seen yet!

If you are looking to have a fun wedding, where your guests will enjoy themselves on the dance floor, and not have to worry about a thing, then this is the guy for you.

We Got Way More Than We Paid For!!!

My husband and I just got married in early October, and we had a large wedding, Steve was an amazing DJ and kept the dance floor full all night. He was great to work with and I was so glad we made the decision to go with him. His prices are reasonable and his quality of work is above reproach. I had so many comments on how much fun was had at our wedding, and a large part of this was Steve and Sound Advice!

You cannot and should not underestimate the role of a great DJ entertainer — they can make or break your special day for you. You can spend your money on flowers or the room decorations and the food can be great; but the one thing people remember is the entertainment - - -how your day was orchestrated from the stage, from the moment your guests begin arriving to the moment the last dance was played — with guests spread out across the dance floor — women's heels off — men's' ties off to one side — everyone exhausted — — — unable to — barely — take — one — more — step.

Time for a Rhetorical Question: Do you want your wedding reception remembered for poor or even just plain bad entertainment or for a great time? Of course the answer is the latter, **a great time!!** One of the recurring problems I see is people don't take the value of good entertainment seriously enough when it comes to planning their weddings or events. I think one of the main reasons for this is the lack of education and emphasis that is placed on wedding reception entertainment and the belief that just anybody can show up and play music at a reception. Fortunately, you know better just by the fact that you are reading this book and taking your wedding reception entertainment seriously.

The Bride and Groom Finally Awaken, However, Not Until the Reception Day

When it comes to the **day of the event**, it is my experience this is the origination of virtually ALL of the stress the bride and groom feels. It is the unknowns stemming from the world of the **DJ Entertainer** where it seems most of the stress factors arise. They realize now, on the day of the wedding reception, they really are not sure who is showing up. The big question in their mind is **who did they really hire** for their entertainment? What is he/she **really going to do**? How is it going to come off when the guests are there and now, sometimes for the first time, they realize: "Oh OOHHHH, It really DOES matter!"

The short term solution – The bride and groom figure they better start paying particular close attention to everything going on so there are no mess-ups. As a result, they are paying less attention to their guests and even less attention to having fun as a newlywed couple. And you can imagine the rest. The bride (mostly) becomes a nervous wreck trying to manage the DJ who is, in turn, trying to manage the reception and the bride. They end up stepping on each other and in the end no one is trusting of each other, neither is talking to the other, both are feeling more and more stressed-out, and each is wondering why.

So, if you want to reduce a huge amount of stress on the wedding day, simply pick a **Great DJ Entertainer** to handle all the unknowns for you during the wedding reception. Consider this person to be your "**partner**" in coordinating the events of the

Resource

Remember to use the
DJ Assessment in Chapter 17
to help you make the best choice for
your DJ Entertainer.
This Assessment is also provided to
you in electronic form in the Toolkit.
By going to
www.WeddingReceptionSecrets.com

day, not simply the lowest cost person you could find to keep spinning the tunes so your guests can dance. The tune-spinner is really only a small part of the day's responsibilities, in fact almost a side job.

What Should I Invest In Quality Entertainment?

Which brings us to the all-important question of how much should you expect to invest in such a person for your wedding reception? There are several ways to address the answer. Some wedding planners and a number of very reputable wedding publications will discuss this topic in terms of percentages of total wedding budgets. I am NOT a FAN of using percentages because the range is way too wide from one part of the country to another.

It also has to do with whether or not the weddings used in the survey had a **Quality Entertainer** or not. If they did not, then their data point will skew the curve significantly and discredit the average in that category. I would much rather discuss ranges, which is what I will do briefly in the next few pages.

And I will call your attention to the "Contact Me" page in the back of this book. It is there for you to use. If this section of fees generates any unanswered questions, then send me your questions and allow me to try to clarify your thoughts.

I know of one wedding where the bride and groom spent about $1,000 on decorations, $50.00 for each plate of food and only $300 for the DJ. Unfortunately, this particular event was over by about 9:00 or 9:30 PM. The hall was gloriously decorated like a senior prom, the food was 5-star in every way yet everybody went home early, leaving most of the great food to waste. If you asked the guests several weeks later, I guarantee they don't remember the food, cake or how the hall was decorated, but they most certainly will remember the $300 DJ who drove everyone out of the room and ended the party early.

Now they have no idea the DJ cost only $300 but they sure will tell you he was really bad or really lousy or really (you fill in the blank here).

Several Examples

If your wedding happens to be in New York City or Los Angeles or a similar cosmopolitan area and in one of the posh hotel ballrooms or country clubs you would likely be paying pretty near top dollar for just about every element of your wedding and reception. We don't need to be exact on the total cost of your wedding but we would probably be pretty close if we estimated a wedding to cost in the $50,000 plus range in these areas   We certainly would not be too far off using this number as our best guess estimate. This is a 100% formal dress wedding. I do not suggest this is a normal or even an average wedding, only a possible higher end wedding and reception investment.

This is an April wedding where there are likely extended cocktail hours in a building removed from where dinner is held. This requires a second set up for sound, music and amplification. It is a very large wedding so dinner extends into two individual ballrooms for an extended time period.

It would not be unusual if this bride & groom had both a DJ and a band to entertain their guests for the evening. Every special dance is conducted; father/daughter, mother/son, first dances, etc. and all the traditional events like cake cutting are adhered to.

Dancing goes well beyond midnight and the DJ is still cleaning up equipment and not getting home until the early morning hours. For a reception like this the bride and groom can expect to invest from $5,000-$9,000 with their DJ Entertainer and Band combined.

Now let's consider an event on the other end of the spectrum. Picture a couple who is having their second wedding. They both already have a couple of grown children and had fancy weddings and receptions the first time around when they were in their 20's. They are now in their 40's and just got married, 6 weeks ago with just their Best Man and Maid of Honor on the beach in Aruba.

Here is their plan for a reception. They are coming home to Boise, Idaho where on a Sunday afternoon they plan to have an informal reception in the park where they have signed up a DJ to play some soft background music for several hours. The purpose is so the bride and groom can welcome their local friends for some light snacks, drinks, cake and conversation. One set of parents is coming in from Green Bay, WI and the other set of parents is coming in from Lafayette, IN.

About 20% of their friends are coming from out of town. Because it is an outdoor event in August, everyone will be dressed very casually and they are hoping for a warm sunny afternoon.

The DJ is a local professional DJ who is charging them from $400-$800 for the afternoon. He has to bring in portable power and transport equipment a fair distance through the park so there is good deal of heavy lifting besides just plugging away at the tunes on the computer keyboard for a couple of hours.

The DJ, who is the Master of Ceremonies for the afternoon, worked closely with the bride and groom in the weeks leading up to the reception. The purpose was to create the plan of exactly what kind of music they wanted and when, to insure he hit all the correct songs and none of the wrong ones. They discussed introductions extensively because there were going to be lots of people from parts of the country who did not know each other and each needed to be introduced properly.

A Midwestern Comparison

Introduction - If you have read the "about the author" section and the "acknowledgements" carefully, or I guess even if you just skimmed them, you probably know by now I am from Northeast Wisconsin, in the Green Bay area. The reason I tell you this is because it's my frame of reference for pricing, for music, peoples likes and dislikes and just about everything else.

I have done a few DJ events outside this core region and in various states throughout the country over the years. The vast majority of the receptions I work are in what I call SE Wisconsin in a general triangle between Green

Bay and Milwaukee and Madison. In general, I know Wisconsin better than I know any other area in the country. It's my home territory.

Now based on this (my) geography, let's present some examples.

Example 1 – Let's say you are looking for a comparison to the DJ in the park in Boise and your goal is to do something similar in SE Wisconsin. If everything were equal, you could expect to invest about the same as this couple did for their Sunday afternoon in the park to enlist a **Quality Entertainer** in SE Wisconsin. Much of the work is in the planning and the preparation for the event. The 2 hours of playing the tunes is really the least of it. It is all the other activities before we ever get to the two hours of playing the tunes where your money is invested big time. It's my preparation using **The Ultimate Forget Me Knot Wedding Planner**™ in **The Ultimate Wedding Review**™ which makes the event look like it was choreographed down to the last introduction and the last song.

We have to qualify this comparison further and make sure we are signing up **Quality Entertainment**. In some cities this is a far cry from just calling on the DJ from the radio station who does weddings part time or the high school DJ. We talked about this extensively in the last two chapters but I do not want us to forget the comparison.

The quoted fee range of $400-$800 is for **Quality Entertainment** in the Midwest too. You can get "cheap" entertainment for far less if you look around a bit, however, I would never suggest such a thing.

Example 2 – Comparing a big city example or a higher end wedding reception to a similar event in SE Wisconsin is a bit more difficult.

I have orchestrated weddings in Wisconsin where we have done every one of the items I described in the New York wedding example back a few pages ago. It was very formal. We did all the dances and all the elements of the wedding. It was big and it was long. I got home very late, etc.

Here's the difference. I did not have to park my van in the loading dock on 5th avenue, get cleared through security, take the service elevator to the ballroom on the 33rd floor to set up for the cocktail hour and then to the 36th floor to set up for dinner. I did not have to arrive at 3:00 PM for a 6:00 PM start time just to get scanned through security to get set up in time.

In one of my more typical locations in the Midwest, I can park at the side door of the hotel, unload using one of my 4 wheel carts and wheel it right into the ballroom on the same floor. It is only a few yards away. I do NOT need to arrive 3 hours early because I do NOT need to get through security at the loading dock in order to use the service elevator to get anywhere! What I am saying is the administration of set-up is far less in most of my Midwestern locations. This substantially reduces the cost. I know many of my readers can identify with this much more simple situation right away.

But building on this Midwestern situation, let's put the cocktail reception and dinner in the same room. Dinner will all fit into one ballroom and after doing all the special dances and all the scheduled reception traditions, the dancing in this case will end as planned at 12:00 PM.

Everything is cleaned up promptly and I am home by a little after 2:45 AM. Whewww!! This wedding is not too far from Milwaukee! Their Investment was in the range of $2,000-$4,500.

My Concluding Viewpoint

I tried to give you the wide range of what you can expect to invest in a Quality DJ Entertainer for a Midwestern wedding reception. I did it by trying to describe a wide range of services you might see a DJ handling at weddings in a metropolitan or more rural region of the Midwestern USA.

No two DJs will have the exact same price structure. It is not like going to the store and comparing the price on 24 oz. jars of low fat Skippy Peanut Butter from one store to the next. Here you know they each will have the same size product because this is all the manufacturer will sell them.

In the DJ world **it is up to you** to sort through the best
and the brightest from those whose elevator does not yet
go all the way to the top floor. Oh, there may be some
signs of life during your interview with them - - - but
remember the reason you go to see each entertainer
perform live. It is because you need to see what they do
when they are under the stress and the strain of the bright
lights and need to perform under the pressure of the bride

Resource

Go get your own **On-Site Viewing Questions** to help
you evaluate talent, along with a variety of other check
lists and tips from Sgt. Steve on the Quick-Start Toolkit
to help you plan your Wedding Reception in the
Appendix of this book.
You can also go directly to
www.WeddingReceptionSecrets.com
and place your order immediately

and groom who is paying them. This is also why you
want to be an avid note taker and use the Resources like
the **On Site Viewing Questions** on the Quick-Start
Toolkit to help you. You want to remember what you
saw this evening, not to get it mixed up with another
viewing you did last Saturday night or this afternoon.

I talk about these On Site Performance Visits in more
detail in the next chapter so I am jumping the gun just a
bit by even bringing it up here. See the Resource Box in
this chapter for details on how to acquire it. There is a
collection of other tools on this toolkit I know you will
want to get your hands on because each one will help you

get a jump start on another aspect of preparing for your reception. Hurry. Do it now.

I hope the discussion in this chapter was helpful for you in providing you some ranges of what you can expect to invest in **Quality Entertainment**. In conjunction with the discussion in this chapter, recall our discussion in the previous chapter where we talked about the risk of "going cheap." THIS IS a totally bad time to try being a coupon shopper. You will get what you pay for. Go **Quality** or don't go at all.

* * ACTION ITEMS * *

1. Determine your total budget for your wedding reception. What is it?
2. Let's Do a Calculation Here. What is the minimum amount you will invest in Entertainment, which will still allow you to have **Quality Entertainment?** Recall! Good entertainment is the #1 thing your guests will remember long after your wedding festivities are over!
3. Let's Do another Calculation Here. What is the maximum amount you will feel comfortable investing in **Quality Entertainment?** Recall! Good entertainment is still the #1 thing guests remember long after your wedding is over!
4. What are those factors that will encourage you to invest more, rather than less to provide **Quality Entertainment** for your guests?

* * NOTES * *

(Please allow me give you a head start here.)

1. *Go to the last two pages in this book and get in contact with Sgt Steve Preston Zuelzke to be the DJ Entertainer for my wedding. I can't wait to meet him in person and get to know him after only reading half of this fabulous book. Wow!*

When It Comes To Selecting the DJ Entertainer for <u>Your</u> Wedding Reception, Remember - - -

You <u>Deserve</u> The Best!

Set Your Sights HIGH and Look For the Pro's Pro

Consider Only a DJ Who
Never Misses a Beat and Will . . .

- Make even the most difficult venues sound great
- Keep the dance floor buzzing all evening
- Know just how to sequence and time your tunes to keep your guests of all ages engaged and having fun every minute of the night
- Keep the children and the young ones entertained and at the same time . . .
- . . . Respect your older guests helping them enjoy the evening with songs they relate to and can dance to with ease
- Guarantee NO breaks
- Use just the right amount of equipment including fog lasers or even bubble machines to delight your guests of all ages
- And of course using just the right mix of lights to meet your every desire

☑ It's Sgt. Steve Preston Zuelzke

The Perfect Mix of Fun, Entertainment and Professionalism, all wrapped up in one package – Guaranteed! *"He is one of a kind"*
CALL: 920-954-0933 or Go To:
www.WeddingEntertainmentGuru.com/Contact

* * NOTES * *

Chapter 7

See Your Entertainment In Advance – Know Who AND What You Are Getting

The subtitle of this chapter could also be:

"Stop The Madness – Pick The Right DJ Entertainer At The Start And You Won't Be Apologizing To Your Family And Guests All Night Long!"

You see - - - - I recommend you go about selecting your DJ entertainment with the same seriousness and sincerity you go about conducting a job interview. I simply mean:

Don't Buy Without a Seeing Each Prospective Entertainment in Person

It's no different than buying a car, really. You need to drive it first. You would never buy a car without seeing it and test driving it first, would you? I dare say you would not!

In the case of selecting a DJ Entertainer or a cover band, however, the industry sometimes tries to push off the old Hollywood Demo & three references on you. Well I am here to tell you that in this day and age, you should not be willing to accept the Demo and reference list as sufficient anymore.

You need to get out and see what you are buying. Yes, just like buying a car.

You Just Cannot Rely On Demo Videos Anymore

A demo video or DVD is just not enough anymore because you never know how old the video is or how much it has been edited in the studio before it arrived at your door. I call some of these just well-done versions of a Hollywood movie. Anybody can put together a demo to make them look a lot better than they do in real life. So until you really see them perform in person, you really do not know what you are going to be getting at your reception.

Won't you be shocked and disappointed when you walk into your own hall on the evening of your reception, with guests arriving, and find out the DJ Entertainer who showed up was nowhere near who you saw on the demo video. When you realize you made a terrible hiring mistake with the DJ or the Cover Band this late in the game, it is too late to change. Yes friend, you are stuck for the evening.

Resource

Go get your own **On-site Viewing Questions** to help you evaluate talent, along with a variety of other check lists and tips from Sgt. Steve on the Quick-Start Toolkit to help you plan your Wedding Reception in the Appendix of this book.

You can also go directly to www.WeddingReceptionSecrets.com and place your order immediately

So if you want to add one more ribbon to your Stress-Free event planning, then please take my strong recommendation here and get out and see (in person and in action) anyone who you are thinking about hiring prior to making your final hiring decision and contract signing.

Then during or right after the visit, take those few extra minutes to document your observations. In other words, take some notes. Just like when you were in school. Put what you saw in writing to make sure you do not confuse one band or DJ with another. It is easy to get bands or DJs mixed up if several weeks extend between visits or if maybe only the bride or groom can get out to see one band or another.

You certainly want to make sure any cover band, entertainment, or DJ you hire can deliver on all of your expectations at your event.

Steve's Sound Advice

Select Your Entertainment Based On Your Own Eyes And Ears, Not From A Video Or Audio Recording

Don't Let a Personal Visit Be a Burden

It may seem like an unnecessary effort or extra burden to find the date and location of exactly where this particular DJ or cover band will be performing to see him or her perform live. Getting permission to visit for a few minutes, traveling (maybe) across town to see them all for the sake of seeing what was on the DVD they already sent you can seem daunting. Remember, we talked about the number of small things you can do to help remove and eliminate the stress from your wedding day. Well, this is one of those LITTLE things you can do far in advance of the day, to eliminate HUGE stress ON your wedding day. You will be VERY happy you did.

Especially in those limited number of cases where you find the video or the DVD **does not match**, you will be thanking yourself a thousand times over for this extra DJ effort.

The rule is, always go to see the entertainment live. The industry will say it's unacceptable and something you shouldn't do. I advise couples and event planners to ask the DJ's and cover band's permission. It's actually a question I have included in <u>The Ultimate Forget Me Knot Wedding Planner</u>™.

You Should Always Be Able To See Them Entertain Live Somewhere.

You want to make sure they are a true professional. Any entertainer should be happy to let you see them live – several times if you wish. If they give excuses as to why you can't see them live, there's something wrong. This should make a big Red Flag shoot up in your mind right away. Find someone else you can go see. It comes back to the smell test for me. If there are too many reasons I can't go see them live, then I begin to wonder, - - "Ummmmm. What are they hiding?" Do I really want them for my reception? What am I going to get surprised with on my wedding day?

I Can Tell You Some of The Things They May Be Hiding. - - -

- ◆ They might have inadequate equipment they do not want you to see.
- ◆ They might have dinosaur equipment looking poor from every angle
- ◆ They might not have the expertise
- ◆ They might not have the professionalism to carry out an event like yours.
- ◆ Maybe they're just watching the computer run (Auto Mix).
- ◆ Are they more concerned about things other than your entertainment- - The photo booth or the up lighting?
- ◆ Did they tell you they are booked out at private events, but really aren't.

The list could go on. You could think of more reasons yourself and for each reason you think of, it's one more reason for both the bride and the groom to invest the time to see this cover band or DJ Entertainer live, in advance, to see if this is what they want to represent them at their wedding reception.

This Is Why You Make On Site Visits! (You Are Going To Think I Am Making This One Up- But I am Not)

Here is another great example of why you absolutely must see what you are getting ahead of time. I was attending a wedding one time where I overheard the "so called DJ" come up to the banquet manager and asked him to pop the garage door to the hall. The banquet manager was stunned and asked why he couldn't just use the normal entrance to the hall to bring in his equipment? The "so called DJ" explained he would like to back his car in to the edge of the banquet hall because his banquet sound system was his car sound system. My jaw slammed to the ground, even though I was just an idle listener, along with the jaw of the banquet hall manager. The hall manager was now in a most awkward position as I am quite sure he had never had this most unusual request before.
Now, had the bride and groom personally visited this DJ before they hired him, I cannot imagine they would have ever considered hiring him if they knew this was his music methodology. Out of the back of his car??? You have got to be kidding!!!! Wow.

The banquet hall manager ended up allowing the DJ to back his SUV into the hall and use the truck's stereo system for the evening as long as the vehicle's engine was not running. Long story short, the bride and groom were beyond dismayed and the whole reception was over by 9:30 PM. I came to find out later this setup, as I suspected, had not been discussed nor were the couple aware the DJ played his music through his truck. Now the bride and groom ended up getting a discount on the fee, but their special day was ruined. No discount can replace a ruined a reception.

You Are a Special Guest When Visiting

Due to the amount of coordination necessary, you must be able to attend the agreed upon date. And always remember you become a guest at the wedding reception, not just an outside visitor. Dress appropriately and behave as you would want a guest to behave at your wedding. And above all, do not overstay your welcome. You are only there to observe the entertainment and draw a conclusion for using them for your reception.

References Can Be Used to See What Is Impossible For You to See

Another issue is references. Say you're from out of town and you want to hire a DJ entertainer, but are struggling with getting in town to see them live. Then you at a minimum need to work extra hard to make sure you get genuine references. You need to get telephone numbers so you can actually speak with someone who has had personal experience with the DJ or the cover band you want to hire. You are **Not** looking for someone who has just heard about them. This is not sufficient. You must talk directly to the person who has hired them for their own event

This is important for you! Remember - - - It's all about doing the little things now to De-Stress your wedding day later! The big payment comes later in terms of saved emotions on your wedding day.

Unfortunately, some companies have been known to make up their own testimonials and use phony references. If you call them on it, they'll tell you they don't have a phone number or email or make some other excuse why it's just impossible to contact the person. You need to always follow up on testimonials and references to ensure they're legitimate and current.

"Current" is an important part of a good testimonial. I see those testimonials or pictures all the time on other entertainers' web sites where the most recent reference is from 10 years ago. My first question is, and yours should be too, "Is that the last time anyone had anything nice to say about them." Or, "What have they been doing since then, huh?"

Doesn't that make you wonder too? Or if they are just too lazy to update their web site, . . . what else are they going to overlook or think is too big of a job on the day of my wedding reception if I hire them?

As you are watching a prospective DJ Entertainer or a Cover Band perform, answer the questions on the Quick-Start Toolkit to help you qualify or disqualify your entertainment. When you print out the list, I encourage you to add your own questions to the document too. You probably have a couple of your own hot buttons about what's important just to you which you will want to include too.

Remember - - - you are hiring the person who is going to be the "behind the scenes" Master of Ceremonies and also your eyes and ears for the evening. This person is going to help create a Stress-Free evening while you are enjoying yourself. **This is a critical position and a critical decision.**

If this is the case, then my advice is to simply go on to interviewing the next DJ. Bad smell and looks are not likely

Resource

Go get your own **Reference Check Questionnaire** to help you evaluate talent, along with a variety of other check lists and tips from Sgt. Steve on the Quick-Start Toolkit to help you plan your Wedding Reception in the Appendix of this book. You can also go directly to www.WeddingReceptionSecrets.com and place your order immediately to change. It is clearly up to you, the bride and groom to be specific as to how you want the DJ Entertainer to dress for your reception event. Don't leave it to chance.

DJ Attire Must Be Appropriate to the Occasion

I've seen plenty of DJ entertainers show up at a wedding or event, in formal wear and look ridiculously over dressed and out of place. On the other hand I have also seen DJ's show up under-dressed, wearing a Hawaiian shirt and flip-flops or T-shirts, jeans, hats or leather vests when this type of garb was totally inappropriate.

At one very elegant wedding I saw the DJ walk up to the bride and her father, wearing a t-shirt with a tuxedo screen-printed on it. They all initially giggled and then the father sternly said to the DJ, "You're really funny. When you are going to put on your tux?" (The sad fact was, this was all the DJ brought to wear on this particular day - He did not own a "real" tux!)

A good rule of thumb to follow is this; if you don't like the way a DJ looks or smells when

Resource

Go get your own **On-site Viewing Questions** to help you evaluate talent, along with a variety of other check lists and tips from Sgt. Steve on the Quick-Start Toolkit to help you plan your Wedding Reception in the Appendix of this book. You can also go directly to www.WeddingReceptionSecrets.com and place your order immediately you first meet him/her, chances are you won't like the way he/she looks or smells at your wedding or event either.

You don't need multiple interviews to verify your intuition.

There Are Critical Questions You Need to Ask When Looking For a Pro DJ Entertainer.

In addition to the details provided in the previous chapter, remember you are best served if you find a DJ who specializes in the type of event you're having. You don't want a radio or club DJ, inexperienced or not properly trained in wedding entertainment, doing weddings. The experienced wedding DJ entertainer knows he/she is not there to be the star of the show. He knows one of his key functions is to make sure everyone is having a good time. Their job at a wedding is to let the music drive the dance floor.

I've seen people hire a cover band or a DJ who they met for the first time in a bar scene to be their entertainment at their wedding. You see you have no idea if this DJ has any experience in doing wedding receptions. It is a totally different type of engagement. One does not apply to the other and this DJ will likely look lost in this different environment. One can only hope in the ensuing interview after meeting a DJ in a bar you can disqualify him/her from doing your wedding by asking the questions from checklists on the Quick-Start Toolkit and the additional details in this chapter.

Remember, wedding entertainment is different from bar entertainment, school, radio or club entertainment events.

You are hiring the person who is going to be the "behind the scenes" Master of Ceremonies and the eyes and ears of the bride and groom. I remind you once again - - -**This is a critical position and a critical decision.**

Ask the DJ about their specialty. Ask them how many weddings they've done. Find out about their background? A good DJ entertainer has the experience and understands the difference in how to run each type event and understands the sub differences of each.

Warning - - -You Don't Want The Radio Or Club Guys Doing Promotions At Your Wedding Or Corporate Event.

I've seen it happen. Yes really! The radio station has their car parked out front with their flashing lights going. He's getting paid to DJ your wedding and promoting the radio station at the same time. How would you feel if this was happening at your wedding? (I think I know your answer!)

"Kind of Ripped Off I would imagine, Right?"

I turn on my "radar." I ask the client to give me a list of songs they and their guests like. I ask them if requests by others are acceptable — and most of the time they are. It's my job to figure out what the couple wants and needs **in advance**. If they tell me their crowd wants oldies and country (but their request list indicates top 40 and classic rock) then I have to work my way through it. But it's why they pay me. It's why they hired me. To work through complications like this.

A Good DJ Evolves As the Evening and the Crowd Evolves

A good DJ entertainer knows the right music to play as the night evolves and as he/she observes the guests evolving too. The DJ entertainer gets paid to insure people are on the dance floor all night long and having fun. To accomplish this, I do not play every request, in the sequence asked. I play some songs longer, some shorter. My objective, as I have said before, is to create a fun environment and to get everyone out dancing. This is a skill and a talent you will not find in every DJ Entertainer, I promise.

In other words, if you give the crowd what they want, they are going to respond and it's going to be a great party. Remember, the DJ entertainer is the "behind the scenes" Master of Ceremonies and the eyes and ears of the bride and groom.

Not Everyone Understands DJ Breaks - There Are None!

Make sure you have an understanding about the DJ taking breaks. **The answer is: None. Period!**

Some DJs I have seen will get two hours into the event; turn the lights on, put on background music and go off to do whatever they want. I have never done this, nor will I ever do it. It is not ethical.

I have seen several events, however, where the **"so called DJ"** in the other hall has the lights on and the music off. I know this because in one case I looked up and saw two brides & grooms and two wedding parties dancing in my hall. I wondered what was going on.

Then the "**so called DJ**" came up to me and asked, "Hey man when are you going to take your break so I can get my crowd back?'

I had to let them know I don't take breaks and "**Him getting His crowd back** was **Not My problem**."

In a couple of cases even the other wedding's bride & groom sent the other "**so called DJ**" home and then combined their party with the event I'm playing at (of course with the permission of my bride and groom.)

Let me be very clear - - -

Professional DJ Entertainers Don't Take Any Breaks!

* * ACTION ITEMS * *

1. Prior to engaging a DJ Entertainer/Band, insure you have a date set to see them perform live. All contracts should include a provision to allow you to see a live performance before any contract is firmed up.
2. During your visit take notes so you do not forget what you observed. Then answer the **On-site Viewing Questions** (See the Quick-Start Toolkit for these questions) and use the results to evaluate how this DJ/Band fits your needs.
3. Make at Least 3 Reference Checks using the Reference Check Questionnaire provided
4. Conduct the DJ Assessment for this DJ. (See the last chapter in this book for these questions)
5. What is the "wedding" experience level of the person you are considering hiring? Remember your wedding is not the high school club or the radio station sock hop. Every DJ is not created equal!

Is It Possible to Find a Professional DJ Entertainer Who is ALSO an Expert Reception (MC) <u>Master Of Ceremonies</u>?

Should You / Can You, Really Set Your Expectations . . .

. . . THAT HIGH?

Well, . . . Let's Set the Record Straight - - -

Not only Should you AND Can you, . . but . . .

. . . YOU DESERVE It!

Yes! That's Right, On This Big Event In Your Life, You Deserve To Have The BEST, The DJ Entertainer Who Has Shown He Is Also An Expert Master Of Ceremonies!

And that's not all. He must also . . .

- Deliver a Romantic and FUN <u>Stress-Free</u> Evening. . .

- Provide Custom Introductions, along with . . .

- Your Personalized Mix of Music – and IN addition . . .

- Meet with you Weeks in advance to <u>Coach</u> You on any Really Tough Reception Decisions . . . AND Of Course

ALL at a Fair Value!

``Who Is This Professional?? Of Course . . . .

 ☑ **It's Sgt. Steve Preston Zuelzke**

The Perfect Mix of Fun, Entertainment and Professionalism, all wrapped up in one package – Guaranteed! *"He is one of a kind"*
CALL: 920-954-0933 or Go To:
www.WeddingEntertainmentGuru.com/Contact

* * NOTES * *

* * NOTES * *

Chapter 8

Stay Away From
the Entertainment Handyman

He has been called "The Jack of all Weddings" or even "The Entertainment Handyman" and the trend continues. More and more novelties keep popping up where brides and grooms get tempted to want to try them at their weddings. As the temptation grows, there will continue to be DJ's who want to add these "tricks" and tools to their wedding kit bags. If you look at it closely, however, all this does is dilute the real mission for which you hire the DJ Entertainer and it's to be the "Behind the scenes Master of Ceremonies" and stage manager for your grand day. These "event novelties" only serve as a HUGE distraction and GIGANTIC misdirection from where you want the DJ's real focus to be: on the music to create a seamless party for you, your family and your guests.

More and more DJ companies (and even some cover bands) are trying to be your one stop shop for everything. The more your DJ messes around with photo booths, up lighting and choreographing entrances, videos, the more wary you need to be about how stretched out he/she is becoming away from their main duties of running the music and entertainment for your event. You should get what you want but make sure you do your homework and hire a qualified expert in each area to handle each area of the technology for you.

These "Entertainment Handymen" DJ companies have lost what their focus is supposed to be. They have gotten lost in what's hot or what is cool at the moment. They need to re-focus back to the real mission, and it's all about the music and entertaining your crowd.

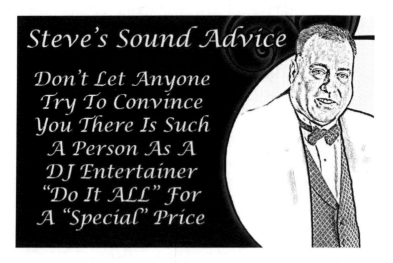

Steve's Sound Advice

Don't Let Anyone Try To Convince You There Is Such A Person As A DJ Entertainer "Do It ALL" For A "Special" Price

One stop shopping sounds nice on the surface. But think about it. Really!! Do you expect your auto mechanic to offer vacations, food and photography? Why do you expect your DJ entertainer to have all of these additional professional areas of expertise? When you come across an entertainment company who promises to do five different things for a couple - - - buyer beware!

I suggest to do a good job they will need a minimum of five different people to run all of what they told you, and chances are they only have one or two people total. Something has to give. It's usually the entertainment. If you're going to hire the all-in-one DJ Company, Here are TWO Key Questions to ask:

1. What is your experience/expertise in any or all other services you want them to perform

2. How many people are on your staff to adequately handle all these services during your event?

Always remember the DJ Entertainer you hired must be focused on entertainment and entertainment only. If you don't feel at all comfortable with the answers given to the above two questions but you still wish to add up-lighting, photo booth, etc., don't just go the lazy route and accept the all-in-one package from the DJ. Go the extra mile to find vendors who are much more equipped to handle these kinds of tasks and let the DJ provide the best possible entertainment.

Picture a one-man band professing to be an orchestra. He's trying to play 27 instruments at the same time. Picture a late-night talk show host being in the control room, running the camera, holding the cue cards and then hosting the show—all at the same time. Chances are he is going to fail at something in this list.

Or look at it this way. Would you hire a DJ Entertainer to provide food and flowers? Then why hire the entertainer to do anything but entertain? A true professional will concentrate on only one thing. Remember you hired them to be the entertainment. One wedding I experienced the bride was upset over the so called everything DJ because the 'up lighting' made the bride's dress looked tan and the wedding party looked like they had bluish pink completions.

The photographer made the DJ shut his improper 'up lighting' off in order to take pictures. Then the bride informed the "so called" Everything DJ she wasn't paying for the 'up lighting.' It made for an awkward rest of the evening since this was the same person doing the so called DJ'ing of the main event (and then the photo booth too).

A Photo Booth Must Be Staffed

I've done weddings where the photo booth person, which must have been contracted directly by the bride or groom, drops the photo booth off then expects me to run it. Wrong! We simply don't have the technology to let anything run on auto pilot for a wedding or event. If it goes un-manned it's not going to be as good as it could or should be. Your guests will not have as much fun as when it is staffed properly.

I have seldom seen additional or alternate entertainment vehicles be effective in a wedding reception environment. It takes away from the real focus of the evening which needs to be on the bride and the groom and their big day. It also takes the DJ Entertainer away from the reason he/she was hired in the first place and remember - - -it's to be the behind the scenes Master of Ceremonies and to coordinate your day!

Don't Get Caught Chasing
the Wrong Rabbits

It seems to me whatever takes the DJ's eye off the main reason she/he's there (the bride/groom) is a reason you want to eliminate these distractions as fast as you can. I now see people trying to cheap out on their DJ in order to afford the up lighting, photo booths or the next trendy gimmick that's in. This is focusing on the wrong things (the wrong rabbits) which are not and will not be memorable. None of them will ever pay off for you in any way for your wedding reception in the short or in the long run. Never. Recall what creates the memories.

It's the entertainment!

* * ACTION ITEMS * *

1. Did the DJ Entertainer or Cover Band make you aware of additional wedding reception services like Up-lighting, Photo Booth, Photography or Videos etc. you had not considered previously? (Circle the ones you discussed) or List additional services offered here_____

2. If any of the above appealed to you, and look like they fit into the theme of your reception, identify suppliers (Not including the DJ Entertainer or Band you are talking with) for each individual service.

* * NOTES * *

Chapter 9

Entertainer Accreditation?
Real Nonsense!

Is your entertainment accredited? What does it mean when a group says they are?

Well, in this industry - - - unfortunately, not much. Actually, it means a lot less than you would hope - - - Nothing in most cases!!

Unfortunately for you the consumer, it doesn't mean anything other than the fact the entertainer has paid their annual dues. To whom? Well, in some cases it means to a membership organization used by talent agencies. In other cases it represents dues paid to professional organizations of which the DJ or entertainer themselves are members. DJ's and entertainers in general have done a poor job making sure their customers really understand what their accreditation means. **Your eyes and ears are the only real judge** of whether an entertainer is worthy of performing at your reception.

Don't be misled by claims of association accreditation. There is no set of standards or a set of tests like a CPA, who has to take some 8-10 exams before they can hang A BIG certificate on their wall and claim to be a CPA. And you are sorely mistaken if you think you have any recourse with an association against an entertainer who breaks their contract with you. No such luck there.

Steve's Sound Advice

Your Own Eyes And Ears Will Be Your Only Accreditation

The following story is a good example of how hiring an accredited talent agency means absolutely nothing. Also another reason to NEVER assume you don't need to see your entertainment live beforehand just because they happen to be accredited. There's a fairly well known cover band here in the Fox Valley, WI area.

They list several well-known associations on their letterhead and in their brochures. They also pay dues to several of the local chambers of commerce and the convention & visitors bureaus in the area. These too are listed proudly in their marketing materials. To the untrained eye all of these names make their resume of memberships look quite impressive. To the trained eye, however, (yours now and mine) this list is just a waste of paper and ink.

They were paid $5,000 for a particular reception. I happened to be doing another job in the same venue downstairs. When I went upstairs to check out what was going on, I found half of the attendees had already left and the other 250 people who remained were huddled around the bar area with the televisions.

I asked the owner of the venue what had happened. He told me the band had been playing so loud they literally blew everyone right out of the room. The band was asked to tone it down but had refused to do anything the bride and groom was requesting. The owner of the banquet facility knew the band members and had worked with this band several times before and even when he asked them to turn down the volume, they refused.

A Band's Ego Can Be What's In the Way

The Band's ego kicked into high gear and I guess because they had the bride and groom's money (and were certainly not looking for any follow up references from them – ever again!), decided to be uncooperative. The band leader actually told the banquet hall owner he'd be more than glad to go home because "I already got my money." He also told the owner he had any more complaints to call his manager.

The reception was over at nine o'clock. In spite of the fact this band came thru an accredited talent agency, which meant to the bride and groom they had a reputation of being honest and trustworthy, they still quit playing prior to the end of their contracted time. It was supposed to go until midnight, but everyone left unhappy at nine o'clock.

The lesson from the story above is simple. Do not make the same mistake this couple did. **Accreditation alone** should NEVER be the only criteria upon which you hire an entertainer **nor an excuse** for not seeing the entertainer perform live before hiring them. And get everything in writing and in the contract.

* * ACTION ITEMS * *

1. For each one of the DJs and Cover Bands you are considering for your wedding reception, list the associations and professional groups of which they are dues paying members.

2. For each one of the DJs or Bands on your list make a call to at least one of their national or state member associations to verify their current membership.

* * NOTES * *

* * NOTES * *

Chapter 10

Working Through a Talent Agency? -- Attention to Detail is Critical

If you decide to work with a Talent Agent instead of hiring a DJ Entertainer directly, I would like to take this time to explain just how Talent Agencies work. There are a couple of things I believe it is important for you to understand before engaging a talent agency to ensure you get the best possible outcome.

First, let's understand a talent agent is much like a sports agent. They represent their client 100% and are out to put them in the best possible situation they can. For starters, you must understand they represent the entertainment industry. They are sales people who provide a brokerage service for bands, clowns, comedians, DJ's and other entertainers.

Think of Talent Agencies Like Sports Agents.

The goal of the sports agent is not only to get their talent paid the most amount of money, but also to get paid handsomely themselves. The same is true for Talent Agencies. They get paid a percentage of the amount you pay for the entertainment you book with them. For instance, if you booked a band through a talent agency and the band charges $5000.00, then the talent agency, would typically earn a 15% commission or $750.00 for the booking. Talent agencies are typically less concerned about the client (you) as they are about the entertainer because they represent the entertainer. The entertainer is their client. This is who they represent. Their number one focus is on making money and they do this by booking their clients with YOU! You are their meal ticket, to put it bluntly. Being the perfect match for you or for your event is never going to be on top of their list of priorities.

Steve's Sound Advice

Electing To Use A Talent Agency Adds More People And Complexity To Your Communication Loop

There are numerous examples of what can happen if you hire a talent agency and are not careful in your negotiations. One couple I knew hired a DJ entertainer but a cover band showed up. When the couple complained, the DJ explained, "There's no one else available this evening, so the talent agency sent me."

If you want a singer, hire a singer. If you want a cover band, hire a cover band. If you want karaoke, hire someone who specializes in karaoke. If you want true DJ entertainment, hire someone who specializes in being a DJ entertainer not just a DJ.

Protect <u>Yourself</u> When Contacting A Talent Agency

Here are 6 key ways to protect yourself when contacting a talent agency:

1. In your first contact be as specific as you can be to let them know exactly what you want. This means you need to have thought through your plans ahead of time.

2. Write down everything implied, stated or promised by the talent agency.

3. Tell the agency you would like all the contract details in writing, in the form of an agreement. At a minimum, the contract should include the:

    a) DJ Service or name of the Band
    b) Name of Contact Person For Your Event
    c) Venue Name, address and room number of the specific Performance room for which you are scheduled.
    d) Time you require the Band or DJ to be set up in the Performance room

e) Start and end times of each event

f) What happens in the case of a No Show? Most Talent Agencies leave the contract as vague as possible in this area because it protects them not you.

4. Meet with the entertainment well in advance of your event (several days to a week or two) to make sure it's a good fit and they will deliver what you want.

5. Require you see their copy of the contract.

6. Pay with a credit card in case of a no show or you don't get what you want. This will be your best protection and one of your best lines of defense if you need it later. (but hopefully you will not)

Resource

Go get your **Talent Agency Evaluation Guide** to help you assess talent agencies, along with a variety of other check lists and tips from Sgt. Steve on the Quick-Start Toolkit to help you plan your Wedding Reception in the Appendix of this book.

You can also go directly to
www.WeddingReceptionSecrets.com
and place your order immediately

When You See the Comparison in Chart-Form, the Advantages of Selecting a DJ Entertainer Direct vs. Working with a Talent Agency POPS Right Out At You

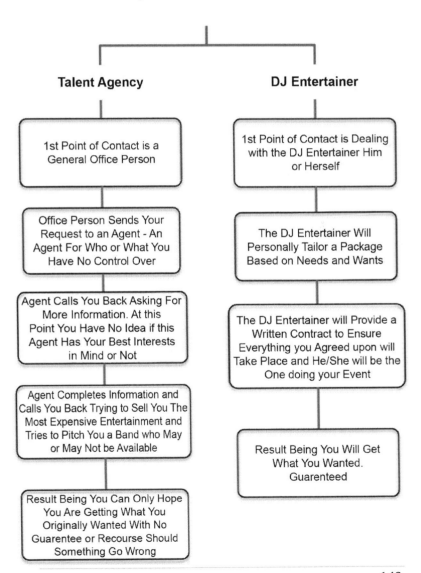

Comparison Between Working with
Talent Agencies versus DJ Entertainers

Talent Agency

DJ Entertainer

1st Point of Contact is a General Office Person

1st Point of Contact is Dealing with the DJ Entertainer Him or Herself

Office Person Sends Your Request to an Agent - An Agent For Who or What You Have No Control Over

The DJ Entertainer Will Personally Tailor a Package Based on Needs and Wants

Agent Calls You Back Asking For More Information. At this Point You Have No Idea if this Agent Has Your Best Interests in Mind or Not

The DJ Entertainer will Provide a Written Contract to Ensure Everything you Agreed upon will Take Place and He/She will be the One doing your Event

Agent Completes Information and Calls You Back Trying to Sell You The Most Expensive Entertainment and Tries to Pitch You a Band who May or May Not be Available

Result Being You Will Get What You Wanted. Guarenteed

Result Being You Can Only Hope You Are Getting What You Originally Wanted With No Guarentee or Recourse Should Something Go Wrong

*The above chart is a clear and easy explanation of the differences between the processes of working with a Talent Agency versus working with a DJ Entertainer.

* * ACTION ITEMS * *

1. Review your contract before you sign it to ensure it specifies everything exactly as you want it.

2. Are you clear about exactly what you do when you want to void the contract should the documented entertainment not be as agreed to?

3. Identify with the talent agency ONE point person who will be in charge of all of your contact for the reception. This will eliminate the confusion and will raise the probability you will get the entertainment you want at your reception.

* * NOTES * *

* * NOTES * *

Chapter 11

Sign the Contract – Success Requires It

Another HUGE secret to reducing YOUR stress for the day of your wedding reception event is to have a signed contract with all the details and all your expectations clearly spelled out so you can focus on having fun with your family, friends and guests.

When you are seeing your entertainment in action before you hire them, you should be taking notes on what your expectations will be for your event. This might be dress, lighting, music, sound, speaker placement, etc. Your notes might also include those items you want to make sure you discuss when you sit down and interview the DJ in person. These are the things you want to clarify or understand better.

In fact, when you sit down with the entertainment service, if they do not provide you with an initial signed contract they have used before, I recommend you simply get up and run the other way. This is a sign they are either hiding something or they are just not very professional. In either case, I would not want to risk having a problem later.

A Contract Defines Expectations

A professional entertainer or DJ company will have a

written contract both parties will sign to seal the deal so both parties understand what is expected of each other. This is a stress reducer for both sides. Like any legal agreement, the contract also protects both parties.

Steve's Sound Advice

Never Ever Move Forward Without A Written And Signed Contract.

Period!

If it is you and I who are working together, then you want to make sure your expectations of my services are detailed in writing, and I want to be sure my expectations of what you are going to do are detailed in writing as well. While it may not seem to be too big of a deal right now, the biggest thing your contract defines is the date of your event.

It protects/identifies the service provider who will show up, where to be, and on what date. It also protects against double booking on the DJ's part.

A few points to make sure you have in YOUR contract include:

- Name of both parties
- Date of the event
- Location of the event – Name or room number of the performance room
- Start time and End Time of Event
- Deposit Amount
- Payment Schedule
- Name of the person showing up at the event
- Name of the package of services you are purchasing – If the package has no specific name then write out in detail exactly what you are buying
- Who is signing this contract and their function in this business
- Date of this contract
- A written guarantee, be specific here. What is it and what is being guaranteed?

Make Sure You Have a Guarantee

A DJ service who is honest and determined to give excellent service will happily give you a guarantee. Any DJ willing to offer a guarantee is likely to give you what you're looking for. It means he/she will back up their promises. The bottom line is this. If you're not satisfied, you should be able to get your money back – but to make sure, everything regarding your guarantee needs to be spelled out in writing and be in the contract!

* * **ACTION ITEMS** * *

1. Review the contract with the DJ Entertainer (A professional DJ Entertainer will take the time to review the contract in person to make sure you understand everything in the contract.)
2. If you did not get an in-person review of the contract, did you understand everything in the contract and did you get all your questions answered before you signed anything.
3. If you feel something is missing, make sure it is added before you consider signing. (If you are still unsure about anything in the contract, never hesitate to consult your attorney.)

When You Select Your DJ Entertainer – SIZE DOES Matter!

Yes . . . It Really Does !!
What Do I Mean . . . ?

The Number of Guests You Invite of Course?

1 - Are You Having a Small Intimate Wedding of Family and a Few Friends
Or
2 - A **Large** Gathering Outside In the Park With Your Families and Guests Joining You From All Corners of the Globe?

- - - So Then, What is the Objective You Ask? - - -

Pick a DJ Entertainer who can customize his set up size, his equipment size, his music, his preparation, his presentation but mostly can customize his style to match the size and style of your families. **You Need to Have a Match!**

So - - Who is your One of a Kind DJ Entertainer Who has been Customizing his Presentation for Years!

☑ **It's Sgt. Steve Preston Zuelzke**

The Perfect Mix of Fun, Entertainment and Professionalism, all wrapped up in one package – Guaranteed! *"He is one of a kind"* CALL: 920-954-0933 or Go To: www.WeddingEntertainmentGuru.com/Contact

* * NOTES * *

Chapter 12

Your DJ Knows Their Equipment . . . Or Do They?

Equipment Does Matter. - - - After All, You Want It to Sound Good . . . . Right?

Most people can best answer the equipment question by judging how it sounds. The main judge is your ears. This is because it is tough to cover up when a DJ or band is using cheap or just plain old or outdated equipment.

I am certainly not suggesting you should know or understand every piece of musical equipment your DJ Entertainer uses by part number or model number. This is far from your line of responsibility. There are, however, a few questions you should be prepared to ask when interviewing potential DJ's about their equipment. Not sure what those might be? Well, don't worry. You will have a much better idea after reading this chapter. I will walk you through the basics of what you need to know about equipment and the importance of actually having live entertainment at your reception.

Resource

Go get your **Equipment Evaluator** to help you assess a DJ's or a band's Equipment, along with a variety of other check lists and tips from Sgt. Steve on the Quick-Start Toolkit to help you plan your Wedding Reception in the Appendix of this book. You can also go directly to www.WeddingReceptionSecrets.com and place your order immediately

The 80's Called, They Want Their Equipment Back

Going Old School might be cool in some things, but not when it comes to your DJ's Equipment. It is absolutely imperative you inquire about just how up to date your DJ's or cover band's equipment is.

Most good bands and DJs are constantly upgrading their equipment and are all too proud to talk about it. They seldom let it get more than a few years old and in fact most are so excited to get into conversations about the newest technologies with anyone who will listen. Always be wary of a DJ or band who gives you vague answers to this question or flat out refuses to give you an answer at all. It's also imperative you make every effort to see the entertainment in person so you can gaze upon the assorted equipment yourself. Part of going to "hear" the band or the DJ is so you can lay your own eyes on his/her equipment in person too. As I mentioned earlier in this book, a DJ will say anything in a meeting to get a booking firmed up.

Vinyl Records Are Still a Thing? – No Way!

I know several people who like to throw on a good classic vinyl on a Friday night to kick back. I'm all for it. Just not at my wedding reception. Any DJ using anything other than computer based sound should be a strike against the DJ. What this means is the DJ has outdated equipment and there is no way it's going to sound good enough for your wedding reception. Period.

You also have a significant risk of some equipment breakdown during the evening. The last thing you need on your big day is an equipment failure. In this day and age of high tech tools and equipment, history can be a pretty good guide. Here's what it tells us.

Anything other than computer based sound and performance equipment is more likely to lead to problems than computer based equipment. You don't have to guess. You can just observe history and take notes. So, one key problem avoidance strategy is to stick with computer based sound and performance equipment. And you certainly are not looking for equipment problems, are you? Of course not!

Look at it this way. Pretend you're going on a cross country road trip. You have a vehicle choice. Do you take the 1999 minivan with 225,000 miles on it or the newest minivan on the lot with only a few miles on it? It's a no-brainer. Throwing on one classic vinyl record or CD at home is one thing. Playing in front of 150-200 people with them is a completely different animal.

If Something Breaks, What Is The Plan?

Any conversation or interview with a potential DJ or Entertainment Company needs to include a discussion about what they intend to do if any of their key equipment breaks during the event. What is their backup plan? How fast can they react and get back up running again? How well they respond to these questions will either make you feel very comfortable or raise a lot of red flags.
The absolute last thing you need to happen on your special day is the DJ entertainer who you hired have his or her equipment blow out during the middle of your reception with no plan on how to get the entertainment back up and running.

This is not the time to take chances. If there is no corrective action plan, then the risk is all on you. Sure, the odds the DJ's equipment will go out during YOUR reception are slim to none, but I know I would personally never hire a DJ or band who doesn't have a backup plan should something go wrong. You shouldn't either. With the equipment & technology available today, anybody can claim to be a DJ.

Steve's Sound Advice

Quality DJ Entertainers Have Contingency Plans For All Equipment Failures.

Does Yours?

Anyone can buy the gear they need. But the BEST DJ's always have a backup plan. They never take their equipment for granted. It is up to you to ask these questions during your entertainment search. Too many bands and DJ's have not asked themselves these questions and most brides and grooms don't even bother to ask during the interview so it never comes up. It just gets swept under the table.

Is It Really Live Entertainment? – Or How Do I Know?

If you were looking to hire a DJ entertainer; how can you make sure you're getting a live body at your wedding and further make sure they're actually going to perform? There's a couple of services in my area who offer iPod/Mp3 weddings. They still, however, call it "live entertainment." They offer it as a $500 live entertainment package. All he/she actually does is set up two speakers on poles and then puts an iPod there and leaves the building. As for my personal definition, I call these "computer weddings." - - - There is nothing "live" about it!

Cost Savings Is Usually Not a Driving Reason

A couple of short years ago, I was the DJ at a wedding in a double hall. Across a large hallway, the groom had decided to take another route for his wedding party and purchased a whiz-bang computer system, rented some speakers and put all the equipment up on stage to play the music for his reception. He had obviously not discussed this ahead of time with the parents of his bride or anyone else in the wedding party because I saw it get pretty ugly. Shortly into the festivities the father of the bride discovered there was no live entertainment.

The groom proceeded to explain to his new father-in-law just how much money he was saving them by buying the computer because he could take it home after the wedding. Unfortunately, his family, friends and guests were not "feeling" the same savings because the vast majority of the party started to head for the door right after dinner about 9:00 PM. They came over to me and asked if they could join our party where I was the DJ. Of course, it wasn't really my party, so I advised them to quickly ask the bride and groom who hired me. The bride and groom of my party were very open minded and congenial about it when they understood the situation and invited them to join us for the rest of the evening.

This is the result if the entertainment consists of an iPod or a computer without an actual human—your event is going to be over around 9:00 or 10:00 PM — guaranteed. It seldom works – and it is never as effective as a real live person coordinating the evening's festivities.

Always make sure there will be a professional DJ entertainer live at your event. Live entertainment means live entertainment. Someone should be onstage, doing the mixing and on the microphone. He or she is driving the event and interacting with your guests all evening long.

There Is Nothing Live About the IPod/Mp3 Player/ Computer Wedding

Be aware of the trend where there is no human involved and the equipment does all the work—which allows the DJ to spend the evening at the bar or to sit in a chair and watch TV or to watch the computer spin. This is what is called an auto mix or some version of an IPod/Mp3 party. The computer basically runs the show. It's hard to call it live entertainment anymore in this instance. Live entertainment is when the DJ entertainer at least entertains on the microphone. It's where the DJ Entertainer does all of his own live mixes and he's making them sound better by what he says in between the songs to relate them to the live audience. When the DJ uses an auto mix program, you'll hear the music but have a lot of trouble finding the Real DJ because he's not there. In many cases it's unlikely he's anywhere near the equipment.

This is no different than having a jukebox playing at your live event. In fact having a jukebox would probably be less expensive. Some companies in my area have a DJ company and yet they offer this IPod/Mp3 equipment rental service under a different brand name. The professional DJ associations I belong to are trying to create public awareness through education of the difference between these two types of events.

One is really a live DJ event and the other is essentially nothing more than renting gear. Be aware when you see ads or marketing for events like this. Much of the wording can still overlap, even still today. What they did was develop a new name, maybe just slightly different from their DJ service name but the contact information is still the same. When they were asked why they were doing this. They replied, "It's still live entertainment, we're just grabbing a different segment of the audience."

The truth was they didn't care and just wanted to make some additional money by tricking some unsuspecting folks.

An IPod/Mp3 Computer Wedding is Simply an Equipment Rental

It is no different than having a jukebox delivered to your reception and then turned on to auto play. Or you might choose to have a relative of yours to bring their home stereo system into the banquet hall and choose some tunes to play. Someone still has to run it and plug in the songs, but in both cases are choosing a non-professional to do the job. You will get the results and consequences you deserve. People won't stay. You will not like the music and you will have minimal dancing. You get what you pay for!

* * <u>ACTION ITEMS</u> * *

1. Ask each DJ or band, when was the last time they had an equipment failure during one of their events and exactly what they did to recover from it? How long did it take to get back up running?
2. Ask each DJ and band, what is their plan of action to recover from an equipment malfunction and how long will it take to get back up and running at my event?

* * NOTES * *

* * NOTES * *

Chapter 13

Room Layout – Why Should I Care?

One of the most underrated parts of wedding reception planning is the layout of the room you are having your reception in. And this relates to how your guests are seated too. Often we don't pay too much attention to these two factors because we don't realize how important they really can be.

Now before you ask yourself why this subject would be of importance or even of interest to you, let me tell you straight. Getting room layout and guest seating correct will enhance the experience for you and your guests for the entire evening. Proper room layout, especially when it comes to sound, will allow each of your guests to enjoy the music at a comfortable level without either being too loud or not loud enough. And you will avoid the constant parade of guests to the front of the room asking for the music to be made louder or softer all night long. I promise!!

Believe ME! It's why I subtitled this chapter, **Why Should I Care?** Just so I could get your attention to what you might think is a dry and mundane topic. But it's not, really!!

Proper Room Set-Up = High Quality Sound

Any really good sound professional will always want to set up so the music will play to the length of the room — never the width of the room. Most banquet halls are rectangular so you'll ideally want the music set up to be focused down the long side of the room. When it is focused to play toward the short side of the room (called playing the width of the room), it's impossible to tune in the sound equipment as well and you will likely get complaints of the music being either too loud or too soft all evening long. It will be a constant battle between the loud spots and the soft spots in the room.

Playing the length of the room will allow for the sound to be much more easily distributed equally throughout the room. It will be loud on the dance floor, and as it travels through the room, the sound will still be at an appropriate level, so people can still hear everything going on and can still talk without shouting at their tables or when walking around.

Room Setup on <u>Your</u> Terms

Many banquet hall owners try/want to dictate how the room is set up for your reception. It may be they have simply "always done it one way or another" and have simply gotten into a routine, for no particular reason. They have their way of setting up the room and since none of their customers have ever questioned them, they assume it's the right way to do things. After reading this chapter, however, you will now know why one layout is better than another. You can have a meaningful, logic-based discussion with them.

Steve's Sound Advice

You Won't Believe Your Ears When The Room Is Set Up Properly

The banquet facility should be able to show you several options. Now it goes without saying, however, in some banquet halls the original architect knew nothing about sound and designed one of those wooden dance floors into a carpeted ballroom. They placed it in a position where they "assumed" the band or DJ would always be setting up alongside of this section of fixed wooden floor. In some banquet facilities this is in the corner. In others it is right in the middle of the short side. In a few I have seen it is appropriately laid in right where it belongs, in the middle of the ballroom floor, allowing maximum flexibility for all events.

It Comes Down To Three Choices

In locations where this section of dance floor has been designed in an incorrect place, you have basically 3 choices as I see it. You can decide

1.) To set the room up in an alternate fashion and NOT use the dance floor for your event, or you can

2.) Use the room as it was designed, in a sub-optimum fashion (which I do NOT recommend), or you can

3.) Select a different venue altogether.

Once you recognize these are the options and you understand what you are getting into with each option, you are likely to hear some push-back from the venue manager. It could sound like, "No one has ever told me this before." Or "No one has ever had a problem with the sound here before." Or "What makes you think your sound will not work like it has for every other wedding reception we have ever had here before?"

At this point it's up to you and you need to decide if you are willing to accept a less than-optimum layout. But there is never a situation where you should accept a layout just because a banquet hall owner or hotel sales manager is just too lazy or too stubborn. The bride and groom (or the event planner) is the customer and should be the ones dictating to the facility owner how they want the room set up.

Most of the time it's simply just a matter of the banquet hall staff moving the tables and chairs around. If the staff is unwilling to do even this simple task, who knows what else they won't do to make your wedding reception the best possible experience for everyone.

Any Banquet Hall Owner and staff not willing to go out of their way to make your experience special is a hall not worth hosting your reception. Period!

Your selection of a particular venue really comes down to two pretty basic things:

1.) Is the Room Layout acceptable, or do you have the flexibility to make it right? and
2.) Is the venue owner or hall manager willing to work with you to make the adjustments so the room is set up to your specifications?

There will be situations where the room layout is fixed where the hall manager has no ability to move permanent fixtures and can do little to help you with modifying the room setup. For instance, his/her hall might one of those designed with the dance floor nailed down on the short side of the room and there is just nothing he/she can do to improve this poor design feature. They just do the best they can with the hand they are dealt. At this point you will have to decide if there are enough other positive factors at this location which allow you to live with the setup (and the resulting sound) as is.

On the other hand, you may come across a facility where the staff has the flexibility to make to arrange a room to your liking but they are just not willing to change the room for whatever reason. They may just be too lazy to do so or they may just have an ego big enough where they refuse to be told what to do and think they have all the answers. No matter what the reason is, any facility that is not willing to go out of their way to make your day special does not deserve your business. Period. Find another place.

I created a diagram to help illustrate my point about how you want to set your room up for the best possible sound by having the music directed the long way down the room. A picture can be worth a thousand words in a case like this.

Whenever Possible, Set Your Music (DJ or Band) So The Sound Is Directed The Long Way In Your Reception Room. In The Picture Below,
This Is In The Southerly Direction.

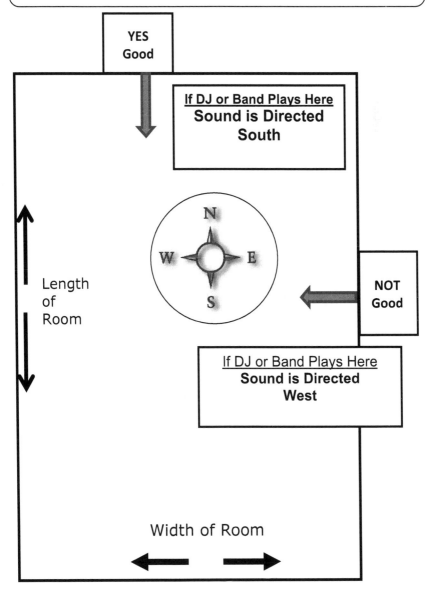

YES
Good

If DJ or Band Plays Here
Sound is Directed
South

Length
of
Room

NOT
Good

If DJ or Band Plays Here
Sound is Directed
West

Width of Room

175

1. **Always** (Or whenever humanly possible) Make Sure Your DJ or band is Set Up to direct their music the Length of the Room. Sound will flow smoothly down the sides of the room so it will be loud enough on the dance floor, and also everywhere else in the room. Guests will be able to hear clearly and still be able to carry on a conversation in a pleasant volume at the tables too.

2. Never, (if humanly possible), allow your DJ to set up to play the width of the room. In this particular instance, the DJ will be right on top of your guests and the sound will blast the ears off of everyone in front of the DJ while everyone off to the sides will be straining to hear anything being played or said at the front of the room.

I hear from frightened clients all the time about how loud it was or how everyone was blown out of the room at another event they attended. Usually it was due to an inexperienced DJ. Hiring a Professional DJ Entertainer with years of experience and having the proper setup of the hall are surefire ways to make sure this will not be an issue at your own event.

Another one of those seemingly trivial issues when you are setting up the banquet hall is exactly how you lay out the room. I have seen this blossom into a HUGE issue during the reception itself when you have not done your studying ahead of time about the importance of proper banquet hall layout. Never settle for less and you'll ensure your reception will be rocking all night long.

Who Sits Where DOES Matters!

Once you have gotten the room layout correct,
it's time to sit down and do seating assignments.
Obviously there really are no rules when it comes to
doing this besides making sure family is sitting with
family and doing the best you can to fit your guests as
best as possible to encourage socialization at the tables.

However, there is one big rule I continue to see being
broken at wedding receptions where I perform. Be kind
to your older friends and family, especially your own
Grandma and Grandpa. I can't tell you how many times I
see older folks seated too close to the speakers. I am sure
this is not done intentionally or but done only to try to
help people with poorer hearing be able to hear the music
better.

The bottom line is the issue can easily be avoided
altogether. Simply have the room set up correctly for
sound and even those folks who are hard of hearing will
be able to hear everything being said and played just fine.
It is a good practice, however, to still sit older people a
little closer to the speakers.

I did a wedding recently where I was ready to start the
dance reception. Grandma was asked to move over next
to me by the wedding couple. She simply refused to
move and insisted on sitting right next to the speakers. Of
course it didn't take long before she was vigorously
complaining about the volume. I explained to her how

the volume would be perfect towards the back of the hall. After awhile she moved. Later in the evening she came back up to me and complimented me on how the volume was so perfect in her new seats after she moved. (What a surprise!)

Please be kind to those older folks at your reception when it comes to sound. After all, they want to enjoy the evening just as much as your younger guests.

Dinner and Cocktail Music Require Different Speakers to Create a Calming Conversation Atmosphere

Your entertainment should have a separate system or speakers for dinner and cocktail music only. This is the professional solution for creating an easy listening, peaceful conversation atmosphere. I find most guests really appreciate this part of the early evening agenda.

When dinner is over you should expect your entertainment to put these small speakers away and replace them with the much larger dance speakers for the dancing and partying part of your evening. Make sure you question your DJ on this during the interview process.

* * ACTION ITEMS * *

1. Is the banquet facility being accommodating to your needs (when then can)? Remember you're the customer and it's your wedding reception.

2. Is the banquet facility and the DJ Entertainer allowing you options (when they can) of how the room can be set up to ensure the best sound quality? (I.e. your entertainment should be directed to the length of the room.

* * NOTES * *

Chapter 14

If a Theme is Important, Go With It!

When it comes to planning your big day, the one thing there is seldom a shortage of is opinions of how to do one thing or another. Your ears will be ringing from all the so called "Know-it-All's" who will be telling you what you should and shouldn't be doing. Additional suggestions on what color to use for one thing and what color to choose for a second area will also be plentiful. Just about no matter who you ask, from family, to friends to people who you hardly know, they will all have an opinion for you on how they would do some facet of your wedding or wedding reception event. And they are all so happy you took the time to ask them.

And when it comes to a themed wedding and reception, you will find those opinions often run even wider and much deeper. And in most cases, you are likely to face various amounts of objection from those who expect a traditional wedding and reception. You will find many who believe your wedding day is not the time to be at all creative or the least bit funny.

But at the end of the day, whose day is it anyways? It's your day. Not anybody else's. Don't let anybody tell you what you can and can't do. It's your choice in the end.

The fact is - - - there is no right or wrong way to do a wedding or reception. It is your day. In my many years in the business, I have seen it all, from 100% straight and narrow traditional to the wild and crazy.

Now obviously your theme, should you choose to do one, should be in good taste and any activities in conjunction with your theme should follow all rules of the facility you are hosting. But otherwise, you should never eliminate a theme from consideration just because some family member or friend tells you not to - - - "just because."

And of course your theme and all of its planned activities still need to be safe and legal. You need to check with the local ordinances and laws in the area where you are having your festivities just to make sure what you have planned is OK to do. I feel compelled to state those obvious words here just so we don't forget to check with the sales manager or banquet hall manager if anything we are thinking about is potentially out on the "skinny branches" of what is safe or in accordance with their hall guidelines and policies.

Steve's Sound Advice

If You've Thought It
Through, Then Don't
Let Those Who Are
Telling You It
Shouldn't Be Done
Stop You From
Doing It!!

I've done many events with themes including weddings.
Some have included Oscar night, NASCAR wedding,
Hawaiian, Hunting, NCAA, Major League Baseball
(MLB) or National Football League (NFL) themes. The
Hawaiian wedding theme was cool. The bride and groom
greeted everyone coming into the wedding hall with a
Hawaiian lei and the hall was decorated like you would
expect to find at a Hawaiian luau. At the NASCAR
wedding, everyone was asked to wear something with a car
brand or their favorite driver on it. If you did not
adhere you were provided a new T-Shirt or hat at the door.

Follow the etiquette you feel comfortable with and
remember to have FUN while doing it. If you pick a
movie theme or a sports team theme there will usually be
a wide variety of formal-wear to fit your event. But be
flexible so everyone can have FUN. In the end it's your
wedding. Themed or not pick a DJ entertainer who will
support what you want to do.

By all means run any ideas past your Best Man, Maid of Honor, your family, your wedding party, and few friends. Get their input. You should be able to trust their judgment. But never let your decision rest on one family or friend who just wants to poo-poo your special day. Obviously in some cases your idea may not work due to restrictions but again, never eliminate a theme from consideration just because some family or friend tells you not to - - - "just because.". At the end of the day, if Theme Is Important....GO FOR IT!!!! If you need someone to support your idea, let me know and we can have a discussion.

* * ACTION ITEMS * *

1. During your planning you need to keep asking yourself: Are all the details I have designed consistent with the overall theme I have selected?
2. No matter what directions you have chosen remember it's your vision. Did you include enough FUN for everyone in each step along the way?
3. If any special activity is planned, verify with the banquet hall owner your special activities are both safe and legal.

* * NOTES * *

* * NOTES * *

Chapter 15

The Ultimate
Forget Me Knot Wedding Planner™ --
Your "How-to" Planner for Your Perfect
Stress-Free Wedding Reception

When you culminate all of you discussions and visiting different venues, it is now time to make sure you have indeed thought of everything. If you had selected me to be you're behind the scenes master of ceremonies, then this is when you and I would be sitting down and going section by section, question by question through **The Ultimate Forget Me Knot Wedding Planner™** during **The Ultimate Wedding Review™**.

When you Pick Steve, <u>HE</u> Is The One Who Takes You by the Hand
<u>From the Beginning of the Plan</u>
<u>To the Final Dance!!</u>

I did a lot of research before we picked Steve and Sound Advice. What I really loved was how Steve was willing to meet with us in person and how he was **the one** who showed up to DJ (<u>not a substitute</u>). He was extremely knowledgeable and so super nice.

The first thing I ask you is about your vision for the day. Some people don't have a vision at all and have not thought at all about the big picture. Sometimes they aren't sure exactly what they're looking for and we have to discuss at length what the possibilities really are. On the other hand there are those who have spent literally years visualizing exactly how they want every single thing to be. Some people already have everything planned out, at least in their mind. They know what they want, but they need **The Ultimate Forget Me Knot Wedding Planner**™ and **The Ultimate Wedding Review**™ to organize it and make it happen. These people quite frequently know their crowd and what their crowd is going to like.

Steve's Sound Advice

The Forget Me Knot Wedding Planner Is Your Building Block To The Perfect Stress Free Wedding Reception

I go through the planning process with them to make the big day for them as easy and as painless and as stress-free as possible. Remember, the goal is to allow you to totally enjoy the day with your family, friends and guests and to not have to worry one little bit about what has to happen at what time during the day. You have handed all of those details off to me.

Again, it goes back to **The Ultimate Forget Me Knot Wedding Planner**™. I ask you a series of questions. I want to know what you want, what you don't want. I want to make sure we are totally on the same page so I am almost thinking like you for the duration of your event. When we walk away from **The Ultimate Wedding Review**™ I have the time line set from start to finish and the only thing left for everyone to do is just have a good party.

After my **The Ultimate Wedding Review**™ I frequently hear a **BIG HUGE** collective **SIGH OF RELIEF** and a big thank you from the bride and groom and/or event planner. I've just given them the ultimate level of confidence. They now feel no matter what happens everything is going to be ok and I have them covered. We have talked about every possible situation and what I am to do.

The final Review brings everything together. It is where all the loose holes are plugged. It creates the time line. It sets the stage for your event and makes sure you and me, your DJ Entertainer, are on the same page, thinking alike, for the event. The more you prepare ahead of time, the better everything runs. It happens every time. Just like in school. The more you study and prepare for the test, usually the better you do, right? It will work the same way here.

I usually find meeting three to six weeks in advance of the event is optimal timing. By this time the bride and groom usually have everything pretty well thought out. In addition, everything else is normally finalized. You're going to have your final number for dinner. You normally know if you are going to be in the bigger hall or a smaller hall. The music charts are going to be pretty much the same when we go in there. We rarely fill in all of the blanks at the final Review, but there still is enough time so you can change things if you wish.

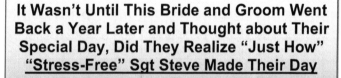

It Wasn't Until This Bride and Groom Went Back a Year Later and Thought about Their Special Day, Did They Realize "Just How" "Stress-Free" Sgt Steve Made Their Day

Dear Steve,
I am going through all my papers from our wedding last September and I am realizing just how great a job you did for us. Thank you for your professionalism and good customer service. If any prospective client ever asks for a reference don't hesitate to send them our way.

Honestly, you were great to work with and we appreciate all you did for us.

Best Wishes-
Andrea

You need to ask your entertainment about their wedding planner tool or maybe if they even have one in the first place. Yes, ask them straight out, like this. "I would like to see a sample of your wedding planning tool." (In the interview process they may only want to only reveal a small sample.)

Now let's get serious here for a moment. I'm not talking about a vague two pieces of paper many call a planner and is really nothing more than a page or two with a few notes scribbled on it with a few steps of what has gone on at previous reception. Some call it a list of ideas and there is almost never a timeline attached. There is little structure and is never any help to you (or them) in structuring YOUR timeline. (If this is all they have, then maybe you should consider booking someone else.)

Compare what you are shown to the things I go through with my clients in **The Ultimate Forget Me Knot Wedding Planner**™. The Planner runs from the before the start of your event to the last dance of your event. It includes, among other points:

- What time are you getting married?
- What time are your guests going to start arriving at the hall? If you tell me dinner is at 6:00 and guests will start arriving at 5:00; I want music playing by 4:45. When the guests walk in the room, the ambiance needs to be already set.
- What is your vision is of a grand entrance?
- Do you want the whole wedding party announced?
- Do you wish to be announced once everybody is sitting down? (or exactly when?)

- Will just the two of you be announced? Every question has more than one option.
- Then there are the first songs of the night. How is the Grand March going to be handled? Certain dances and songs. When? These questions all need to be asked.
- Do they want me to play the Hokey Pokey or The Chicken Dance or The Macarena? Are those on the "play" or the "do not play" list?

I create the list and then guarantee, yes guarantee, the clients I will make sure whatever they asked for on the list will be delivered. — They can walk away and not have to worry about it. I guarantee it. This Ultimate Review Meeting only takes between 30 and 45 minutes. It is the best way possible to prepare for your actual event. After our final Review, I will try to contact you every week, and at least one week before your event. Why? Because I want to maintain our communication and see if anything has changed. In addition, there is often a short list of items each of us is following up on as we lead up to the event and I want to be checking on the status of each of those open items insuring they are getting completed and closed off the list.

All of my clients have almost unlimited access to me by my office, cell phone and email which goes to my smartphone. So as we are leading up to your event, one never needs to have a question go unanswered for more than an hour or two.

When it comes to song selection, I have almost any song you want for your specialty dances. However; don't expect your crowd to go wild over something they don't know or have never heard before. Based on my many years of wedding reception experience, people at a dance reception want to hear the songs they either know or can dance to. Playing a bunch of songs no one knows is going to achieve one thing - - - - - a bare and empty dance floor. I have no problem playing songs the bride and groom want played, but I will also make sure to use my expertise at this final meeting to make sure the play list is appropriate.

I don't play songs with questionable language. No reputable DJ Entertainer will. It's my policy as it will be for all DJ Entertainers. Your Grandma will be happy to hear all of my music selections. And all of my music is ready for radio airplay. If you're dealing with a DJ Entertainer who has no issue with playing inappropriate music at your reception, I would suggest you're hanging out with the wrong crowd or you need to cross this DJ off your list.

At a recent reception I played at, the bride and groom wanted me to play Crazy Bitch by Buckcherry. I was reluctant but it was 11:45PM with no children still there and the groom wanted it. In this case I felt if I'm going to play this song the timing was right. I put the song on and the place erupted. The dance floor packed and I wish I had videotaped grandmas and grandpas fist pumping and yelling the expletives. It was a crazy end to a good night. If you're going to have "questionable" songs on your list,

then at least use some common sense as to when they should be played.

Just remember, if you choose to play any "questionable" songs even if they don't contain vulgar language, you better know your guest list. The timing worked out for this bride and groom but others may not be so lucky.

At the end of the day, I know I've done my job and it makes everything worthwhile when I get compliments during the event and at the end of night. Some people even come up to me in tears telling me what a wonderful time they've had. And to top it all off, I give the bride and groom a special wedding gift. Why you ask? I say this because this day is all about the bride and groom. It's my way of saying thanks to the couple for selecting me to help make their special day just a bit more special.

To me, it's exactly what a good DJ Entertainer does. In fact it is one of the qualities OF a top Quality DJ Entertainer. And hopefully after reading and using this book, you now realize it takes a little more effort to find an excellent DJ Entertainer who focuses on YOU, but it is so much more worth your effort. The payback for your time and money is HUGE!!!

* * **ACTION ITEMS** * *

1. Does the checklist/planner tool lay out the total road map for your wedding reception and help you begin to see your total vision for the day?

2. During the interview process have you had a chance to review the checklist you are going to use at your review meeting 2-3 weeks before your wedding reception?

3. Does the checklist appear to be a comprehensive list including each of the major components of your wedding reception, like a song list for cocktail hour separate from the dance portion of the evening?

Are You The Bride or Groom . .
Who Needs to Have Every Detail Planned

- To the minute - - with no stone left unturned
- Every reception puzzle piece **neatly wrapped up – well in advance . . .**
- And in place for you to sleep well and feel like you are **ready for the big day**?
- And you want a DJ Entertainer who is patient, appreciates you and will not get bored . . .
- . . . Working **with you on EVERY detail.**

☑ If – YES, This is You - You Found Your Guy

☑ It's Sgt. Steve Preston Zuelzke

1. Sgt. Steve is NOT the DJ who just shows up on the night OF and Plugs IN! no No NO!
2. He starts weeks ahead - - - Just Like You Do Introducing his expertise and lending you his sought-after **Ultimate Forget Me Knot Wedding Planner**™ ···

- **His Patented Tool** (No one else has it!), which
- Answers ALL the key questions
- About Every Phase of Your Reception
- Based on his Years of Valued Experience
- So Nothing is Missed or Overlooked
- No Loose Ends – which . . .
- . . .Removes All The Reception Stress and strain. - - - When? – Before it happens!!!
- And NO Left Over jumbled to-do lists like you have heard from other friends and brides

- - - Think of how it will feel to be **"Sleeping Like a Baby"** in the days leading up to your wedding because every detail is nailed down!.

☑ It's Sgt. Steve Preston Zuelzke

The Perfect Mix of Fun, Entertainment and Professionalism, all wrapped up in one package – Guaranteed! *"He is one of a kind"*
CALL: 920-954-0933 or Go To:
www.WeddingEntertainmentGuru.com/Contact

What Would It Mean to Your Stress Level if YOUR DJ Entertainer Came to the Table With a Checklist... So All You Have To Do is Decide Which Steps Apply To Your Event

Steve,

We cannot thank you enough for our wedding and everything you did to make it so special and memorable. You were incredibly easy to work with despite living so far away while trying to plan everything. Your excellent services and professionalism were key factors in making our special day go off without a hitch. I would definitely recommend you to anyone who is looking for a first-class party or event.

Giving us the sound recordings of the entire evening was especially generous and will help us relive our most precious memories.

Lastly, your detailed planning and expertise in the field relieved an immense amount of stress and strain on our brain. Thank you again so much for everything! You truly are a top-notch DJ and go way above and beyond to separate yourself from the competition.

Thanks a million!!
Brandy and Matt

Sgt Steve Preston Keeps the Bride and Groom
Smiling and Having Fun At their Wedding Reception
<u>all the Way Thru till the Last Dance</u>

On a July night, Sgt Steve Kept this Happy
Couple Smiling all the Way till the Very
End of their Reception in Appleton Wisconsin

* * NOTES * *

* * NOTES * *

Chapter 16

The Ultimate Wedding Review™ -- Your Final Review Discussion to go Over Every Detail of the Wedding Reception

Flying by the seat of your pants is never the way to go when it comes to your wedding reception. It is just way too important of a day to leave anything to chance, especially when there is time to actually plan out all the details. Most of us have at least one GPS app on our smart phone and another GPS in our automobile which we use to get directions to even a nearby store when we are not sure of the location. Right? We don't leave a short trip as trivial as this to chance, so why leave the planning of something as "un-trivial" as your wedding day to chance? Right? Of course not!!

I've heard about impromptu weddings and receptions, and I always think to myself, "Ummm - - - they must be in Las Vegas, and they must be in a hurry." Being in Las Vegas, to me, would be about the only acceptable reason to rush a wedding and/or reception without any proper planning. The total lack of planning is much more of a sign of laziness than it is a lack of understanding. We all know we should do it and we all know roughly how to do it.

Any professional DJ entertainer, and I emphasize the word "professional", DJ you select should take you by the hand and sit down with you (no matter what type of event, but most especially when it is your wedding) and guide through you each step of the way to plan your wedding reception event from beginning to end.

A true professional will make your planning experience almost as fun as the reception itself. To help create the experience for the bride and groom, I take every client through **The Ultimate Forget Me Knot Wedding Planner**™ Tool during the Ultimate Wedding Review™. I take every bride and groom through the entire evening and nail down every single detail of their wedding reception from the moment the first guest arrives until the last song is played and the lights are turned off on the dance floor.

The Ultimate Wedding Review™ will go over every

Music Selection is a Key Part of Your Successful Planning Process

Sgt. Steve,

Thank you for the excellent performance. We had a great time! Many people complimented us on the music selection in which you were a very big help in us selecting the right music.

Thanks also for the recordings.

Mike and Terri

detail of your wedding reception from the cocktail hour to the last dance. We will leave no leaf unturned as we plan every facet of your wedding reception day together.

We nail down every detail, exact timing, every song selection, yes everything. I want us to do the hard work, together, up front so you can 100% enjoy your day, Stress-Free, with no worries. Remember, I will be your behind the scenes master of ceremonies and stage manager to carry out your every wish.

Steve's Sound Advice

Remove The Uncertainty And Indecision From Your Reception Timeline And Make Sure You Don't Leave Anything Out, With An Ultimate Wedding Review At Least Two Weeks Before The Wedding

If the DJ entertainer you select does not take you through this type of pre-planning, then you are missing some things altogether. Other items you are skimming over and in general you are just leaving way too many key activities to chance. That's a guarantee!

Hey – It's your Wedding Day, not a trip to the ballgame!!

Without **The Ultimate Wedding Review™,** your event coordinator goes into the event not knowing **exactly what YOU want.** They might pull out their cheesy props or start with old, dated dances because they are just guessing what you really want. Would this be upsetting to your family, friends and guests? Is this what you would want to take place on this most important day, just because no one asked you the questions?

Picture this: The DJ is running after the bride and groom *during the reception,* (I call this the DJ puppy dog syndrome). He is carrying a notepad and a pad of paper asking them the very questions he should have asked them during **The Ultimate Wedding Review™** at least two weeks BEFORE the reception (which never happened).

Tonight is when you, the bride and groom, should be **enjoying yourselves,** having fun with **your family, your friends and your guests. You should NOT be** answering these kinds of trivial questions. It's **your wedding reception** and you should be enjoying yourself! It is SO… SO… important your DJ entertainer insist you have a wrap up **Ultimate Wedding Review™** at least two to three weeks <u>before your reception,</u> to set the final time line and make all the final decisions. If your DJ does not demand this meeting or even offer the opportunity then you need to be the one to insist the DJ sit down with you to create the important time line. Never accept "Oh, we'll be okay. I have everything written down. No need to meet a few weeks before." If that's the response you get, your Major RED FLAG meter should be going off like fireworks immediately.

(Note: – This would be one of my make it or break it questions on whether I selected this DJ or not!!) You hired your entertainment to be much more than somebody who just shows up to "spin tunes" at your reception. You hired them to be your Master of Ceremonies and Operations Manager for your reception. A professional DJ Entertainer will not take this task lightly and will be prepared to walk you through your entire evening, several weeks before hand.

If your entertainer does not use **The Ultimate Forget Me Knot Wedding Planner**™ or some type of pre-planning questionnaire, I would seriously consider looking elsewhere for your DJ Entertainment. You, as a couple have so much more you need to be dealing with before

You Will "ONLY" be Thrilled With How the Reception Goes, When Your DJ Has Helped You Plan it All Out Ahead of Time

Dear Steve,

We wanted to thank you for your awesome DJ services at our wedding. We were absolutely thrilled with the way the reception went and it's all because of you! We have had many compliments on your services and people are still talking about you! Thank you so very much! Please thank your son as well. You guys make a great team.

Yours Truly,
Karen and Brian

the big day, trying to figure out which questions to ask shouldn't be one of them.

Your DJ Entertainer should have the entire list of key questions prepared FOR you, in an effort to make your reception be much easier and Stress-free. Keep in mind, creating the right set of questions to ask is a huge job and a gigantic responsibility for the DJ Entertainer. Don't take on this level of planning when you can leave it to an expert. Thinking of the right questions is one of the main reasons you hire the DJ Entertainer in the first place.

It is one responsibility I would strongly advise against you taking on, at the same time as you are trying to plan your wedding. It is just too much for a bride and groom to have to deal with at this time of their new life together. It has taken me over ten years to perfect my list of questions.

Folks, here is one of the major reasons, and quite frankly, why you pay a little bit more to hire the "best." Then you get "The **Best DJ Entertainer**," who comes **with all the tools already tested and ready to apply to your wedding reception.** This is what allows you to have a Stress-Free day, knowing you have picked the right DJ Entertainer / partner to be the behind the scenes master of ceremonies to carry out all of your wishes and desires for the event. You get to sit back and be the beneficiary of a DJ entertainer who has done it before, has the answers for you and knows how to improvise for you when something doesn't go just exactly as planned.

My **Ultimate Forget Me Knot Wedding Planner**™ not only asks the right questions but it also helps avoid some very uncomfortable situations and unpleasant surprises. One such situation was an interracial wedding I played at early on in my career. Let me tell you, I was *Ohhh Sooo Not Prepared.* Now by the end of the evening I was able to overcome some difficulty and was successful in getting the crowd to mix, mingle and have a fun time.

Nearing the end of the evening, I asked the mother of the bride why she had not let me know about the interracial nature of the wedding when we were engaged in **The**

Ultimate Wedding Review™ several weeks ago? "This is how," I explained, "I uncover special issues like this so I can do a thorough job of preparing my music prior to the show."

Her answer could have knocked me over with a feather!

She said. "I never brought it up because you never asked!"

I do now.

Another great example was a wedding where I was the DJ a few years ago. This time it involved the parents of the groom who happened to be divorced.

We had started playing the dinner music. Dinner was being served. The manager of the banquet hall had just started to pop the top on the champagne and the pouring team had begun to take their stations and begin their task for the evening. The mother of the groom went over to the person pouring champagne and told them, in spite of some bottles being opened; she had earlier in the day cancelled the order for champagne. There was "No way she going to pay for it."

The father of the groom, who was there with his girlfriend, and just happened to be within earshot, stood

up and said, "I reordered it and I will pay for it, so please sit down."

The mother of the groom started to yell back "You were never there for me" and went on and on. The groom then stood up and yelled across two tables, "I told the both of you I didn't want any of this shouting at my wedding so both of you please just sit down and chill out. Remember whose day this is.!!" (He used much worse language, I assure you.)

. . . . .You could have heard a pin drop.

But talk about the awkward silence!!. Wow!

If I would have known about these relationships ahead of time, I could have tried to run some interference and tried to help avoid this very tense situation from ever starting in the first place.

But you can bet your bottom dollar I now ask the bride and groom about any potential problems or extenuating circumstances we might need to be aware of due to any strained family or guest relationships. I do it during **The**

Ultimate Wedding Review™ several weeks before the reception.

By having this discussion early and talking about these potential situations, I force the bride and groom to think this stuff out long before the wedding reception. This allows them to be much better prepared for any potential 'blow ups' that might occur during the reception. Let me tell you, it makes the evening a lot less awkward the more prepared the DJ Entertainer and the couple hosting the reception can be when possible blow-ups might occur.

The bottom line is the more prepared the couple is as well as the DJ Entertainer, the more successful your reception will be.

You'll be amazed at how relieved you will feel after thinking and talking all this through BEFORE your special day. And your DJ will be far more prepared to handle any unforeseen situations you <u>have not discussed</u> when you have talked about those you think might actually arise the night of you reception.

As you have probably heard it said before. Make sure your talk about "The elephant in the room."

It's your night. When you are prepared, you can Have A Great Time With Family and Friends and Guests!!!!

When the DJ Takes the Time to Create a
Plan with You, Only Then Do
You Guarantee Yourself a Great
Evening

Dear Steve,
We wanted to send you a big thank you for doing such a great job at our reception! Everyone really enjoyed themselves and had a lot of fun all thanks to you! You were so helpful helping us pick the music and made good choices for all the other dancing music. We really appreciated that.

We also want to thank you for the recordings you made for us, We weren't expecting that at all! It was really nice of you!! We listened to them the other day and relived the night over and over again. It's so great to know we'll always be able to relive the night of our wedding forever!
Thanks again for making our reception one we'll always remember!!

Jason and Leah

You Too Will Be Smiling at The End of Your Forget Me Knot Wedding Planner Review Knowing <u>Your Entire Evening Is In The Hands of a True Professional DJ Like Sgt Steve Preston</u>

This Happy Couple Is All Smiles Knowing Their Worries and Stress Have Been Relieved After Meeting with Sgt Steve For The Ultimate Wedding Review in November 2015 at BJ Clancy's in Appleton, Wisconsin

Skepticism Turns to Glee For This Husband 'to-be' When The <u>Results of The Forget Me Knot Wedding Planner Review Finally Hit Home!!</u>

When Heather told me who she had selected for our wedding entertainment, I was at first a bit skeptical. My skepticism came from all of the great things she had to say about you and your service. **It just sounded too good to be true.** I quite frankly didn't think any service or anyone one could be THAT good. Within a Very few minutes after meeting you, however, you changed my mind. I was quickly impressed and very confident you were all she told me you were. You came across as the real expert at doing weddings.

I told Heather, "Wow! I have to compliment you on making such a great choice for our wedding entertainment." After our Forget Me Knot Perfect Wedding Planner Review was complete, I was so confident and relaxed everything would be handled exactly the way we want and knew I could concentrate on just having fun."

Heather & Eaitan Maoz-2015

* * **ACTION ITEMS** * *

1. A Quality DJ Entertainer will show you an agenda for the Final Review Meeting during the initial interview process. Have you seen this agenda from each DJ and Band?

2. Does the contract with your DJ or band set a date at least two to three (2-3) weeks before your reception to have a review of each of the details of the entire wedding reception step by step?

3. Based on how your interview and early contacts with this DJ and/or Band leader have gone, what is your assessment on this person's style and/or ability to coordinate and conduct this final review meeting 2-3 weeks before your wedding reception?

Your Wedding Entertainment Experts at Sound Advice. From your first Planning Meeting all the way thru the Last Dance, This duo will help Coordinate <u>YOUR Special Evening Every Step of the Way</u>

Son Steve and Sgt Steve Preston are getting ready for another Stress-Free Wedding Reception in Appleton, Wisconsin

You Will Never See Anything Other Than the Most Current and Up to Date Equipment at a Sgt Steve Preston Event

At this Green Bay Wisconsin Wedding, Sgt. Steve is Keeping People Dancing from the First Song to the Last

* * NOTES * *

Chapter 17

The DJ Entertainer Assessment

Note: This Assessment is also found on the Toolkit

How do you know if you have selected the best DJ Entertainer for the most important day in your life? Well, until now you didn't. Lucky you! Now there is a simple 24 question assessment for you to use to judge one DJ entertainer against any other.

Steve's Sound Advice

The DJ Assessment Will Put Your Mind At Ease You Are Hiring A Quality Entertainer For You Wedding Reception

When to use this assessment tool:

1. The best time to use this DJ Entertainer Assessment tool is during the planning phase of your wedding reception event. Don't wait until you are into the details of picking out the songs and signing the contracts. *It's way too late.*

2. Answer the assessment questions prior to any contracts being signed with the DJ Entertainer. You want to know this person is the right person to be

working with before you are locked into working with him/her.

How to get started:

1. Just put a checkmark by the Yes or No after you read the following 24 statements as they apply to this DJ Entertainer you are considering for your wedding.
2. After you have completed all 24 questions, add up the number of questions to which you replied Yes.
3. Use the scoring system after question 24 to assess this particular DJ Entertainer.
4. How did they do? Is he/she a keeper?
5. If you have a winner, then get the contract signed and get on with the planning process - - - - pronto!!
6. If, on the other hand you have a loser on your hands then you have two choices to make.
   a) First you may simply decide to part ways and move on to your second choice of DJ Entertainers. This is actually the easy choice. If you make this choice, then do it and get a move on, quickly.
   b) Or second, you might look at the scores and determine this DJ is so close in a number of items you feel you really could work together with a little bit of improvement. So you decide to coach this DJ up to "winner" status in these areas.

If this is your choice then put your coaching cap on tightly because time is of the essence. Your wedding date is getting close so look at which items in the assessment are "No's." Create a mini-coaching plan, present it to the DJ and get moving with the initial steps right away. Best wishes on your plan.

Here is the 24 Statement Assessment

From a People Perspective

1. In setting up our first introductory meeting, the DJ Entertainer respected our wishes, communicated with us in the way we desired and got back to us in a timely fashion.   Yes _____   No _____

2. We held our Face-to-Face meetings in locations which led us to believe we were working with a true professional business person.
                            Yes _____   No _____

3. The DJ Entertainer was dressed in such a manner which led us to believe we were working with a true professional business person.
                            Yes _____   No _____

4. The DJ Entertainer was attentive to our wants and ideas for our reception but at the same time, offered us good feedback and was engaged in helping us plan the best reception possible. We had good two way communication.   Yes _____   No _____

5. In my continued meetings with the DJ Entertainer, he/she showed increasing proficiency and expertise in wedding entertainment which gave me increasing confidence I had picked the right person to plan my reception with.   Yes _____   No _____

6. Not once during our meeting did the DJ Entertainer use his/her membership in the American DJ Association as the main selling point of why we should do business with him/her.

   Yes _____ No _____

7. The DJ Entertainer showed us the cover sheet to his liability insurance policy to verify he has all the appropriate coverage just in case anything goes wrong during my event. Yes _____ No _____

From a Process Perspective

8. The DJ Entertainer requires a deposit from me to assure our date is being held in their calendar and they will not double book. Yes _____ No _____

9. The DJ Entertainer is willing to accept my deposit and lock in our date as far as 2 years out in advance (if necessary). Yes _____ No _____

10. The DJ Entertainer took the time to inform me of any possible event conflicts with our first choice of dates we picked and worked with me to find a good alternative (if necessary). Yes _____ No _____

11. The DJ Entertainer gladly visited my reception venue because he/she had not played there before and was anxious to see the layout, understand the technical requirements, meet the owner and understand any nuances of working an event there for the first time.

    Yes _____ No _____

12. The DJ Entertainer was open to having us attend a scheduled event they are working so we can evaluate him/her in action.   Yes _____   No _____

13. I came away from our meetings believing the DJ Entertainer is solely focused on being the best Master of Ceremonies as possible. Not even once did he/she try to sell us add-ons such as up lighting or photo booth.   Yes _____   No _____

14. The DJ Entertainer schedules a face to face **Ultimate Forget Me Knot Wedding Review**™ to take place 2-3 weeks out from our reception to review and firm up the event timeline and to ensure all objectives will be achieved.
                Yes _____   No _____

15. The DJ Entertainer took the time to explain proper room setup so I understood best sound quality.
                Yes _____   No _____

16. The DJ Entertainer explained in detail his backup/recovery plan should anything happen to him that would prevent him from performing at my wedding reception on the appointed date at the agreed upon time. I am comfortable my event will still be adequately covered.   Yes _____   No _____

From a Product Perspective

17. The DJ Entertainer gave us an overview and showed us the basic equipment they will be using at our event.
Yes _____ No _____

18. The DJ Entertainer made it crystal clear how they would be using quite different speaker/broadcast equipment for the softer dinner/cocktail music than they will be for the main dance portion of the reception music. Yes _____ No _____

19. The DJ Entertainer made it absolutely clear they have backup equipment should something go wrong and the backup plan was fully discussed during our meeting. Yes _____ No _____

20. We were presented with a written contract from the DJ Entertainer which laid out everything we discussed and clearly explained what is expected from both parties. Yes _____ No _____

21. We went thru the entire contract line by line in a face to face meeting to make sure we understood everything. Yes _____ No _____

22. The DJ Entertainer utilizes "**The Ultimate Forget Me Knot Wedding Planner**™ as a valuable tool we can use together to plan out all the details of my stress free reception. Yes _____ No _____

23. The DJ Entertainer provides us a Wedding Reception Etiquette book as another valuable tool for use to help guide us through virtually all of the key procedural or etiquette decisions I need to make prior to our reception.   Yes _____   No _____

24. The DJ Entertainer offers us a Quick-Start Toolkit containing checklists and assessments (in electronic form) to help us get a jumpstart on planning our wedding reception. It includes a HUGE variety of handy time-saving checklists to make sure we don't forget anything and to help our reception be as smooth and as stress free as possible. Yes _____ No _____

Let's Finish Up:

♦ Review the Assessment and add up all of your Yes's

♦ Mark Your Total Number
            of Yes's Here   _____

♦ Now See How This Candidate Fares on the Evaluation Guide on the Next Page

This DJ Entertainer Scoring:

Number of Yes's	Evaluation Guide
Less than 12 = 50%	Inadequate – Run the other way, and Make it fast.
13 to 17 = 60%	They are a year away. Not ready for your wedding reception but if they are serious about practicing their craft they could be the ones to improve their performance in the future.
18 to 20= 75%	Marginal – However, depending on which questions are the No's, it might be worth sitting down to see if any of the No's can be turned into a Yes with some work. Coaching several of the No's into Yes's are a real possibility, however, you should also have a backup DJ ready as an option. Have a discussion with this DJ who you are going to try to coach to determine if this strategy is feasible and will be well received. Will there be time to still be able to work with this person?
21 to 22 = 90%	A real possibility. Just one or two Yes's away from being a Winner. It is clearly worth trying to correct several No's and turning them into a winning Yes.
23 to 24 = 100%	Winner - You have a real winner here Sign the contract and don't let this one get away.

This DJ Entertainer Final Score _____

Date of This Assessment _____

Name of Candidate _____

* * NOTES * *

Appendix

Hear It From Others –
More Happy Brides And Grooms

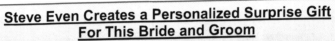

Steve Even Creates a Personalized Surprise Gift For This Bride and Groom

Steve,
We wanted to say Thank you for doing such a wonderful job at our wedding reception. You did a fantastic job and everyone had a great time!! The music, lights, and bubbles were all a hit.
The snowball dance was also a great idea, everyone said how much fun they had!
Thank you very much also for the recordings of the songs that were played. It is something we can listen to and remember how much fun we had!!

Thanks again!
Eric and Kelly

When You Work With Sgt Steve, The Compliments You Receive On Your Reception Will Never End

Steve,
Thank you for a wonderful evening of music. To say we had a wonderful time would be an understatement.
Everyone who sees us tells us how much fun they had celebrating our special day. Thank you for your contribution and playing the Piano Man encore.

Carrie

You'll be hopping to a wide variety of music with Sgt Steve

Dear Steve,
Jason and I would like to thank you for playing music for our reception. You played a variety of music to get the crowd on the dance floor. Many people complimented me on my choice for a DJ. Thank you also for the musical recordings of our dance. Listening to it brings back fond memories!

Thanks,
Jennifer and Jason

We Are Ready to Call Steve When We Are Ready To Renew Our Vows. .

We tied the knot in April. We didn't leave much time for our wedding planning. As soon as we chose our DJ which was Steve he made the entire music portion of it a breeze. I thought there was going to be a lot and really was a breeze. He has awesome quality, knows how to have a good time and really know what he is doing. I was really happy after choosing him and I got lots of compliments from our wedding party. Steve also took time to make us a special gift on our wedding day, which was totally unexpected!!! If and when we are to renew our vows I will definitely be calling Steve up!!! Thanks again Steve for your awesome DJ service!!!!

Steve Helped This Bride and Groom Have Many Fond Memories of Their Special Day

Steve,
Thank you so much for providing the music at our wedding reception. We received many wonderful compliments from people saying how much they enjoyed the variety of music, lightshow-the whole package!! We had a wonderful time dancing to all the music-You made it fun for everyone!!

Thanks Again,
Brian and Kathryn

Steve Created a Stress-Free Environment For This Bride and Groom

Sound Advice-
Thank you for doing such an amazing job at our wedding. We received a lot of compliments on how awesome you guys were and can't thank you enough for making the evening a fun, entertaining worry- free event for us!

Dan and Jesse

Steve is Flexible and Comfortable In ALL Environments

Dear Steve,
Thank you again for being such a great DJ for our wedding! You played so many great songs that we and many of our friends and family literally could not leave the dance floor!! Thank you for putting up with my younger brother's constant requests.   You were very nice to him!!!

We appreciate the Recordings of our reception. We will now be able to re-live our special day at anytime thanks to you!! We will refer you to anyone we know who needs a DJ!!!

Kristen and Brian

This Couple Had Such a Great Experience With Steve, They Are Looking Forward To Hearing Him Again at Another Friend's Wedding Reception

Steve,
You did such a great job at our wedding! We had a blast listening to the recordings on our ride back to Colorado. I know Stu's Parents can't wait to get their hands on the tapes to listen to them too. Didn't get a chance to give you a tip-so we enclosed one.

Can't wait to hear you again in December.

Thanks Again,
The Londy's

Appendix

See It From Other's Point Of View:

Everyone, Including the Wedding Party, Is Enioving the Chicken Dance

Wedding Guests Enjoying the Chicken Dance with the Wedding Party in Hollandtown, Wisconsin

Steve can be your Theme Wedding Coach
Just Like He Was For This Couple

Another Successful Theme Wedding
in Hollandtown, Wisconsin with Music by
Sgt Steve Preston and Sound Advice

Guests of ALL AGES feel Comfortable
on the Dance Floor When Sgt Steve Preston
is YOUR DJ Entertainer for the Evening

Guests of All Ages, including Grandpa at this Kelly Lake
Wisconsin Wedding Enjoying the Music All Evening Long

Appendix

Index

A

Accreditation 9, 139, 142
Action 71, 117, 153, 162, 221
Afternoon 82, 88, 105, 106, 107, 110
Agency 9, 69, 140, 141, 145, 146, 147, 150, 243
Agent 145
Assessment 9, 217, 218, 219, 243
Association 51, 139, 220
Atmosphere 41, 73, 89, 178
Attire 124

B

Backup 161, 162, 221, 222, 224
Band 67, 68, 69, 70, 71, 73, 74, 75, 77, 87, 89, 104, 105, 115, 116,
     117, 118, 120, 122, 123, 125, 135, 140, 141, 145, 146, 147, 159,
     160, 162, 171, 176
Banquet... 5, 44, 49, 50, 55, 56, 57, 60, 61, 75, 77, 120, 121, 141, 165,
     170, 171, 172, 173, 176, 182, 207
Break 82, 88, 100, 128
Bride 23, 41, 42, 44, 57, 58, 70, 72, 75, 87, 89, 95, 101, 103, 104, 105,
     106, 110, 117, 120, 121, 124, 126, 127, 128, 135, 136, 137, 141,
     163, 172, 183, 189, 190, 193, 194, 202, 204, 206, 207, 208
Budget 8, 50, 55, 56, 57, 58, 59, 60, 64, 92, 95, 97

C

Calendar 49, 55, 220
CD ...89, 161
Checklist 20, 243
Cocktail 19, 70, 75, 89, 104, 108, 109, 178, 203, 222
Computer 106, 119, 160, 161, 163, 164, 165
Contact 10, 69, 77, 92, 103, 122, 147, 165, 192

Contract.. 9, 22, 50, 117, 139, 142, 147, 148, 153, 154, 155, 218, 222, 224

Couple... 43, 51, 76, 101, 105, 106, 107, 121, 123, 127, 128, 134, 142, 145, 146, 163, 177, 194, 209

D

Dance 11, 22, 40, 72, 73, 75, 82, 84, 89, 100, 102, 104, 125, 127, 170, 171, 172, 176, 177, 178, 191, 192, 193, 202, 203, 222

Decorations... 100, 103

Dine.. 42, 83

Dinner. 20, 59, 61, 70, 75, 89, 104, 108, 109, 163, 178, 190, 191, 207, 222

DJ 6, 7, 9, 11, 18, 19, 20, 21, 56, 67, 68, 70, 71, 72, 73, 75, 77, 81, 82, 83, 84, 85, 86, 87, 88, 89, 90, 91, 92, 97, 98, 100, 101, 102, 103, 104, 105, 106, 107, 109, 110, 115, 116, 117, 118, 120, 121, 122, 123, 124, 125, 126, 127, 128, 133, 134, 135, 136,137, 139, 145, 146, 147, 150, 153, 154, 155, 159, 160, 161, 162, 163, 164, 165, 171, 176, 178, 183, 189, 193, 194, 201, 203, 204, 206, 207, 209, 217, 218, 219, 220, 221, 222, 223, 224, 243

DVD 116, 118

E

Engagement... 125

Entertainer...6, 9, 11, 18, 21, 56, 67, 68, 70, 71, 72, 75, 81, 82, 83, 85, 86, 87, 88, 89, 91, 92, 100, 101, 102, 103, 105, 107, 109, 115, 116, 119, 120, 121, 123, 125, 126, 127, 133, 134, 135, 136, 139, 142, 145, 146, 147, 150, 153, 159, 161, 162, 164, 176, 183, 189, 193, 194, 201, 203, 204, 206, 209, 217, 218, 219, 220, 221, 222, 223, 224

Entertainment ....1 , 4, 6, 7, 8, 9, 10, 12, 16, 18, 20, 21, 42, 44, 49, 50, 55, 56, 67, 68, 71, 72, 74, 75, 76, 77, 81, 82, 83, 95, 96, 97, 98, 100, 101, 102, 107, 108, 111, 115, 117, 118, 119, 121, 123, 125, 126, 133, 134, 135, 136, 137, 139, 140, 145, 147, 148, 153, 159, 160, 161, 162, 163, 164, 165, 178, 190, 219

Entrance... 120, 191

Equipment .. 6, 9, 89, 90, 105, 106, 119, 120, 159, 160, 161, 162, 163, 164, 165, 170, 222

Etiquette 183, 223

Evaluation.. 224, 243

Evening......22, 61, 82, 86, 87, 88, 89, 90, 97, 104, 110, 116, 121, 123, 127, 136, 146, 160, 163, 164, 169, 170, 178, 202, 207, 208, 209

Experienced..56, 125, 135

F

Facility 56, 57, 141, 171, 172, 182

Family .. 5, 8, 39, 40, 41, 42, 43, 44, 58, 73, 86, 88, 115, 133, 153, 163, 177, 181, 182, 184, 188, 204, 208, 209

Father 104, 124, 163, 208

Flag 76, 77, 119

Flowers 55, 95, 96, 100, 135

Food 40, 41, 50, 56, 57, 58, 92, 95, 96, 100, 103, 134, 135

Forget Me Knot 9, 51, 107, 118, 187, 188, 189, 191, 202, 207, 221, 222

Fun 1, 17, 42, 44, 51, 73, 101, 127, 136, 153, 202, 204, 207

G

Grandma 177, 193

Groom 19, 20, 23, 41, 42, 44, 57, 58, 70, 72, 75, 87, 89, 101, 103, 104, 105, 106, 110, 117, 120, 121, 126, 127, 128, 136, 137, 141, 163, 172, 183, 189, 190, 193, 194, 202, 204, 206, 207, 208

Guest 18, 50, 56, 58, 95, 121, 169, 194, 202, 208

I

Ipod 164

Item 18, 57, 60, 71, 86

K

Karaoke 67, 73, 74, 147

Knot 58

L

Location 42, 43, 49, 89, 118, 155, 201

M

March.. 70, 75, 192

Maximum... 60, 61, 171

Midwest... 74, 108

Minimum 73, 74, 121, 134, 147

Money....... 11, 16, 18, 20, 21, 51, 60, 81, 96, 97, 100, 107, 141, 145, 146, 155, 163, 165, 194

Mother.. 105, 207, 208

Mp3 .... 163, 164, 165

N

Notes 117, 153, 161, 191

O

On-line 241

P

Parents...6, 40, 55, 57, 58, 105, 163, 207

Party ... 5, 18, 39, 40, 43, 51, 60, 82, 88, 103, 127, 128, 133, 136, 163, 164, 184, 189, 191

Person....... 21, 22, 24, 57, 72, 73, 83, 84, 85, 86, 92, 95, 97, 102, 115, 116, 117, 122, 123, 126, 136, 147, 153, 155, 160, 164, 208, 217, 219, 224

Photo 119, 133, 135, 136, 137, 221

Plan....... 8, 23, 40, 52, 58, 88, 95, 105, 106, 161, 162, 201, 202, 203, 206, 218, 219, 221, 222

Planner 9, 18, 23, 51, 107, 118, 172, 187, 188, 189, 191, 202, 207, 222

Priority 97

Professional 5, 75, 81, 85, 86, 87, 91, 106, 119, 128, 134, 135, 139, 153, 164, 165, 170, 176, 178, 201, 202, 219

Publication 4, 58

Q

Quality............56, 73, 87, 102, 103, 107, 108, 109, 111, 169, 194, 221
Question..40, 56, 57, 89, 100, 101, 102, 118, 122, 159, 160, 178, 187, 192, 217, 218
Quick-Start 110, 123, 126, 223, 243, 244

R

Reception.. 9, 10, 16, 21, 22, 24, 39, 40, 41, 42, 43, 44, 49, 50, 51, 56, 57, 60, 64, 67, 69, 70, 71, 72, 74, 75, 85, 86, 87, 88, 90, 91, 96, 97, 100, 101, 102, 104, 105, 106, 108, 109, 111, 116, 119, 120, 121, 123, 136, 137, 139, 140, 141, 153, 159, 160, 161, 162, 163, 165, 169, 170, 172, 173, 176, 177, 178, 181, 182, 187, 191, 193, 201, 202, 203, 204, 206, 209, 217, 219, 220, 221, 222, 223, 224
Record 161
Reference.. 106, 115, 122
Rental... 164, 165
Reputation 6, 11, 68, 69, 141
Review.......9, 21, 55, 88, 107, 187, 188, 189, 190, 192, 201, 202, 204, 207, 209, 221

S

Secret 68, 153
Standard... 44, 86
Stress... 1, 4, 9, 16, 17, 42, 44, 45, 52, 55, 58, 60, 87, 91, 97, 101, 102, 110, 117, 118, 122, 123, 153, 154, 187, 188, 203, 206, 222, 223
Stress-Free .9, 16, 17, 44, 52, 87, 91, 97, 117, 123, 187, 188, 203, 206
Success 9, 153
Surprise 58, 81, 178

T

Talent 9, 23, 69, 127, 139, 140, 141, 145, 146, 147, 148, 150
Theme 9, 181, 182, 183, 184
Toolkit 10, 110, 123, 126, 217, 223, 243, 244

U

Ultimate 9, 51, 71, 88, 107, 118, 187, 188, 189, 191, 192, 201, 202, 204, 207, 209, 221, 222

V

Vendor 5, 78
Venue......8, 43, 44, 50, 51, 55, 60, 92, 95, 96, 140, 141, 147, 172, 220
Video...67, 72, 73, 116, 118, 133
Vision 187, 191
VJ 67, 72

W

Wedding 1, 5, 8, 9, 10, 11, 16, 18, 19, 21, 22, 24, 39, 40, 41, 42, 43, 44, 49, 50, 51, 55, 56, 58, 59, 60, 61, 64, 67, 68, 69, 70, 71, 72, 74, 75, 81, 85, 86, 88, 90, 91, 95, 96, 100, 101, 102, 103, 104, 105, 107, 108, 109, 118, 119, 120, 121, 122, 123, 124, 125, 126, 128, 133, 135, 136, 137, 153, 160, 162, 163, 164, 165, 169, 172, 173, 177, 181, 182, 183, 184, 187, 188, 189, 190, 191, 193, 194, 201, 202, 203, 204, 206, 207, 208, 209, 217, 218, 219, 221, 222, 223, 224
Wedding Planner 9, 18, 51, 103, 107, 118, 187, 188, 189, 190, 191, 202, 207, 222
Wisconsin.. 106, 107, 108

ATTENTION!!
YOU Just Completed <u>This BOOK</u>!

<u>YOU</u> Have <u>Received Amazing Value</u>
And <u>Incredible Help</u> In Planning <u>Your</u>
Wedding Reception Entertainment
From This Book - - - And Now There
Are Others Who You Want To Help the
Same Way.

What About Your . . .?

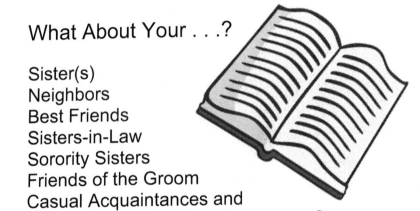

- ◆ Sister(s)
- ◆ Neighbors
- ◆ Best Friends
- ◆ Sisters-in-Law
- ◆ Sorority Sisters
- ◆ Friends of the Groom
- ◆ Casual Acquaintances and
- ◆ Those You <u>Really</u> Want To Impress?

Of Course You Want to get <u>Each</u> of your friends their Own
Book because of this very **SPECIAL** Offer Only
AVAILABLE Here at My Web Site!
You won't find it on Amazon or anywhere else on line!
(Order 3 books and get 1 Free plus Free Shipping)

Just Pick up your black ink Pen or Pencil and fill in the
Order Form on the next page. Then Fax it to me at
920-954-0933 -- Or you can go directly to the on-line
Order Page at: **www.BestReceptionBook.com**

☐ YES, I want to order **ADDITIONAL COPIES OF:**

Discover...The "How To" Secrets of Planning Your Wedding Entertainment.

I have received so much help in planning my wedding reception and so many benefits from this fabulous book, in such a short time. Thanks Sgt Steve. I have to get my hands on more copies for **my friends** who are planning their wedding entertainment right now. I understand **my investment now is only $22.97 plus $3.95 Shipping or one Free when I order 3 (and Free Shipping).**

Today's Date	
Order Quantity	█████████
Name	
Address	
City, St. Zip Code	
Phone	
Fax	
Email	
Credit Card Type	____ Visa ____ MasterCard ____ Amex ____ Discover
Credit Card Number	
Credit Card Expiration Date	Month Year: ████████
CSC Code	Total $$ to Charge
Signature to authorize payment(s)	

Fax a copy of this entire completed page to me at 920-954-0933
Or Go to **www.BestReceptionBook.com**
to Order On-Line immediately.

ATTENTION Serious Readers of:

Discovering The "How-to" Secrets of Planning Your Wedding Entertainment

To Help You Get The Full Value From This Book, I have created a set of Extra Resources waiting for you on the

Quick-Start Toolkit
At:
www.WeddingReceptionSecrets.Com

It is a set of Word Documents Including your:

1. DJ Assessment
2. Venue Assessment Guide
3. Reference Check Questionnaire
4. Talent Agency Evaluation Guide
5. DJ and Band Equipment Evaluator
6. In-Person Viewing Questions
7. Wedding Reception Vendor Status Checklist
   Plus More there wasn't room to list here!!

Save yourself *DAYS* of research and development time. Get this set of **pre-made tools** to help you get a jumpstart on what you need to ask in each situation.

Plus: a **Bonus 15 minute One-on-one** Telephone Conference Call with me, Author Sgt. Steve on my private line.

☐ YES, I want to order the Toolkit. **RUSH it to me!**

Discover...The Wedding Reception Secrets
- Quick-Start Toolkit

You talk about the many powerful resources, tools and checklists in this Toolkit so often in this book I have just got to get my hands on the Real Thing. I understand as long as I am an owner of the "Secrets" book I can buy at the amazing discount for this companion Toolkit. For **non-book owners the price is $69.97**, however, as a **book owner, my investment today is only $14.97.** Wow - That's **a whopping 78.6% discount.** If you don't own the book yet, either fax in both order forms or order them together on-line. It's that easy.

Today's Date	
Order Quantity	██████████████
Name	
Address	
City, St. Zip Code	
Phone	
Fax	
Email	
Credit Card Type	____ Visa ____ MasterCard ____ Amex ____ Discover
Credit Card Number	
Credit Card Expiration Date	Month Year: ████████
CSC Code	Total $$ to Charge
Signature to authorize payment(s)	

Fax a copy of this entire completed page to 920-954-0933 OR to order on line, go to www.WeddingReceptionSecrets.com

ᴧᴦTENTION Bride and Groom:
You Got HUGE Value From <u>This Book</u>

But Wait . . . There's More!! Take the <u>Next Step</u> to
Ensure Your Wedding Reception Is <u>Stress-Free</u>,
and <u>Empty-of</u> Any Embarrassing <u>Moments</u>
Grab a hold of Sgt Steve's "2nd" Book . . .

"12 Wedding Reception Courtesies
You Need to Know! - - -
- - - Ignore Any One of These and Your Reception
Just Might Be Remembered For All the Wrong Reasons"

This 2nd book is the **ONLY ONE** ever written to let you in on each of
those **12 wedding reception courtesies, or manners** as our parents
called them. Many brides don't discover these until it is too late. So late
and they have now become an embarrassment to them at the reception.
Sgt. Steve details all **12 of these manners** for you Right here in one
place. These are the same **P's and Q's** your Mother has been dropping
you little hints about the last year, but you have not been paying too
close attention. This book will let her know you really have been
listening to her and make her proud. So here is your chance to get all
these little, yet HUGE, decisions made ahead of time so you can have a
stress-free and a "no-worries" day. **Order this book Now**!

What About Your friends who have weddings coming up right after yours?
Remember your sisters, cousins, friends, neighbors and buddies of the
groom who you want to impress.

How Many Do You Need?
Get **each** of your friends a **Book-** (**They'll be thanking you!!**)
Let's make it an **easy decision with an "Over-the-Top Offer."**
You won't find this offer anywhere else, even on Amazon!
(Order 3 -- Get the 4th Free, Plus Free Shipping)

Just Pick up your Pen or Pencil and fill in the Order Form on
the next page. Then Fax it to me at **920-954-0933**.
Or go directly to the on-line <u>Order Page</u> at:
<u>www</u>.DiscoverStevesTips.com.
The books will be heading your way pronto!

☐YES, I want <u>Sgt Steve's</u> **NEW 2nd book**, Right Now

"12 Wedding Reception Courtesies You Need to Know! - - -

- - - Ignore Any <u>One</u> of These and Your Reception <u>Just</u> <u>Might</u> Be Remembered For All the Wrong Reasons"

I am so excited to have discovered this new book today. What a **Great Find**! I need to get this book now so I can avoid any possible embarrassing moments at my wedding reception. It's JUST what I Need! I am ordering **additional copies for my friends** too, who are starting to plan their receptions next month. I can't believe my investment now is Only **$12.97 each plus $3.95 Shipping OR**, <u>Free Shipping</u> **and 1 Free Book when I order 3.**

Today's Date		
Order Quantity		
Name		
Address		
City, St. Zip Code		
Phone		
Fax		
Email		
Credit Card Type	____ Visa ____ Amex	____ MasterCard ____ Discover
Credit Card Number		
Credit Card Expiration Date	Month	Year:
CSC Code		Total $$ to Charge
Signature to authorize payment(s)		

Fax a copy of this entire completed **page to me at 920-954-0933** OR go to www.DiscoverStevesTips.com to Order On-Line.

Appendix

How to Contact Me, the Author

To contact me directly, Sgt. Steve Preston Zuelzke, the author of this book, please send an email to
SgtSteve@TheWeddingEntertainmentGuru.com

Put **SECRETS BOOK** in the SUBJECT of the email so I know you are a reader of this book and I can respond to you as my priority customer.

Thank You

Monthly Drawing!

If You Own This Book, Then You Can Win Again!

As You Prepare For Your Big Day, What Would It Be Worth To You If You Could Win 30 Minutes of Sgt Steve's Valuable Time To Get Your Most Pressing Questions Answered In A One-On-On Conversation With The Expert Himself?

When you got this book, besides receiving the obvious wisdom of the book itself, you also earned the right to enter into a **BONUS Monthly Drawing.**

What Exactly Do You Win?

Each Month Steve is giving away a 30 minute one-on-one coaching call. That's Right, a **Half Hour** of his Valuable **Consulting Time.** Time he usually charges over $1,000 per hour for, so you can get your most nagging reception questions answered by the guru himself. That's Sgt. Steve Preston!

But That's Not All!!

Along with the Monthly Coaching Drawing, Steve is will be giving away a **$100 Hotel Gift Card** to another lucky winner. So you have two chances to win every month. This gift card is good at hundreds of hotels across the world.

Also at least once a year

Steve is going to reach a little deeper into his Bowl of Prizes and pull out a:

2-Day Post-Honeymoon Get-Away Cruise!

This will leave out of a Florida port and is available to everyone, even if you have won before.

How Do You Enter?

Just go to:
www.BestReceptionBook.Com/Drawing

and fill in the form. Tell Steve your name and address, and when and where you purchased or received this book. Once you enter you are in for good. No need to re-enter. – and of course Steve never sells or gives your name away under any circumstances, never!

Hurry! Get your Name in before this Month's Drawing

When It Comes To Selecting the DJ Entertainer for <u>Your</u> Wedding Reception, Remember - - -

You <u>Deserve</u> The Best!

Set Your Sights HIGH and Look For the Pro's Pro

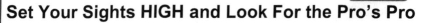

Consider Only a DJ Who
Never Misses a Beat and Will . . .

- Make even the most difficult venues sound great
- Keep the dance floor buzzing all evening
- Know just how to sequence and time your tunes to keep your guests of all ages engaged and having fun every minute of the night
- Keep the children and the young ones entertained and at the same time . . .
- . . . Respect your older guests helping them enjoy the evening with songs they relate to and can dance to with ease
- Guarantee NO breaks
- Use just the right amount of equipment including fog lasers or even bubble machines to delight your guests of all ages
- And of course using just the right mix of lights to meet your every desire

☑ It's Sgt. Steve Preston Zuelzke

The Perfect Mix of Fun, Entertainment and Professionalism, all wrapped up in one package – Guaranteed! *"He is one of a kind"*
CALL: 920-954-0933 or Go To:
www.WeddingEntertainmentGuru.com/Contact

63860613R00138

Made in the USA
Charleston, SC
15 November 2016